In our world of shifting s Psalm 11:3 comes to mind: 'If what can the righteous do? eternal answers of Scripture His potent and succinct presentation of God's truth will undergird your faith and remind you of just 'how firm a foundation' belongs to those who build their worldview on the unmovable bedrock of the wisdom of our Lord Jesus Christ.

Peter A. Lillback
President, Westminster Theological Seminary,
Philadelphia, Pennsylvania

A Christian without a biblical worldview is like a sailboat on tempestuous waters, foolheartedly dashing into waves with wide-open hatches. Too many Christians are in peril and don't even know it. Don't be a double-minded man and easy prey for the world, the flesh, and the devil. Read this book, meditate on the eight truths Pastor Pacienza presents, and build your faith on a firm foundation.

Rosaria Butterfield
Author, *Five Lies of Our Anti-Christian Age*

Rob Pacienza has provided us with a potent Christian worldview primer in the space of a very few pages. Practical, insightful, rich, and inspiring, this is a book every pastor, every teacher, and every parent needs in their arsenal of truth during these challenging days in which we live.

George Grant
Pastor Emeritus, Parish Presbyterian Church,
Franklin, Tennessee

Rob Pacienza's *How Firm a Foundation* is bold, urgent, and pastoral. In a world where shifting cultural tides threaten to erode biblical convictions, he provides a much-needed anchor for the soul and issues a clarion call for Christians to stand unwaveringly on the infallible Word of God. With clarity, depth and wisdom, Pacienza unpacks eight essential truths that fortify believers against the storms of relativism, secularism, and moral confusion. This book is a roadmap for living with courageous faith in an age of compromise.

J. Ligon Duncan III
Chancellor and CEO, Reformed Theological Seminary

Research shows that only a small percent of Christians have a biblical worldview—holding beliefs consistent with what the Bible teaches. If every self-identified Christian understood and believed the foundational truths contained in this book, it would completely transform the church. This is a clear, concise, and accessible guide to the indispensable truths every Christian should know. I wish I could put it in the hands of every believer today.

Natasha Crain
Speaker, podcaster, and author, *When Culture Hates You*

This readable book helps develop the structure of a Christian worldview so necessary to live faithfully in a shifting culture. Jesus ended His Sermon on the Mount with a story about two men, one building a life on the sand the other on a rock. Foundations matter. Read this book to strengthen your own faith and then share it with a friend.

Erwin W. Lutzer
Pastor Emeritus, The Moody Church,
Chicago, Illinois

We live in unusually tumultuous times, where changing currents seem to be moving faster than we can catch them. Believers and unbelievers alike often find themselves scrambling for purpose, meaning, and security amidst the ever-shifting sand beneath their feet. In this very readable book, Robert Pacienza provides an introduction to some of the key Christian ideas which offer the firm foundation many seek, including creation, the sanctity and meaning of life, sin, truth, and the divinity of Christ. Whilst these may seem like "ordinary" ideas to most Christians, Pacienza helpfully pitches them against some of the ideologies and social issues which cause so much of the confusion and despair in our time, offering prophetic, pastoral, and practical exhortations for Christians to speak truth boldly where it is most obscured, to take action where necessary, and an encouragement for sceptical unbelievers to look deeper at the claims. *How Firm A Foundation* offers sound, biblical encouragement thoughtfully applied to everyday life, helping to guide the discouraged, the sceptical, and the wave-beaten alike back to the eternally secure rock of Christ and His Word.

Aaron Edwards
Author and theologian

ROBERT J. PACIENZA

HOW FIRM A FOUNDATION

EIGHT TRUTHS
FOR AN
UNSHAKEABLE
FAITH

CHRISTIAN
FOCUS

print ISBN 978-1-5271-1270-4

ebook ISBN 978-1-5271-1330-5

10 9 8 7 6 5 4 3 2 1

Published in 2025

by

Christian Focus Publications Ltd.,

Geanies House, Fearn, Ross-shire

IV20 1TW, Great Britain.

www.christianfocus.com

Cover design by Tobias Designs

Printed and bound by
Bell and Bain Glasgow

FSC
www.fsc.org

MIX
Paper | Supporting
responsible forestry
FSC® C007785

To the students of

Westminster Academy (Fort Lauderdale, FL).

May you build your lives upon the firm foundation of Christ Alone!

Contents

Preface

"How Firm a Foundation" has long been a popular hymn, especially in the North American church. Charles Hodge, the great Princeton theologian, was so overwhelmed by the fourth verse that he could only gesture the words.[1] It speaks of the unshakeable nature of our faith in Jesus Christ. In an increasingly secular age, the church needs to be reminded of this sure foundation.

The truths surveyed in this short book are not exhaustive of the Christian faith, but certainly foundational. My goal was not only to provide scriptural support for our beliefs but also to show the uniqueness of Christianity and the counter-cultural nature of the biblical worldview. Living in a society hostile to Christ should not cause us to fear, but instead cause us to respond with a humble confidence, knowing that the truth will always prevail.

I want to express my appreciation to the congregation of Coral Ridge Presbyterian Church. It is a joy and honor to serve them as their pastor. I am also thankful for my

---

1   Tim Challies, Hymn Stories: How Firm a Foundation, Challies, March 17, 2013, https://www.challies.com/articles/hymn-stories-how-firm-a-foundation-free-download/.

good friend, Dr. Rita Cefalu. Her editing and proofreading of this book have been invaluable. We are grateful for her contributions as Scholar in Residence and Senior Fellow at the Institute for Faith and Culture. Likewise, many thanks to Dr. Laura Groves for serving as copy editor. She has been helping me to be a better writer ever since high school English.

May God embolden us to live out a faith that will not be swept away by the cultural winds. This will not be done according to our power, but according to the same power that raised Jesus from the dead. My prayer is that you will be encouraged to build your life on the one thing that is immovable—the infallible Word of God. It is our only firm foundation.

> How firm a foundation, ye saints of the Lord,
> Is laid for your faith in His excellent word!
> What more can He say than to you He hath said,
> To you who for refuge to Jesus have fled?

A Biblical Worldview

The essential starting point for building a firm foundation is to develop a truly biblical worldview: a worldview based upon the Word of God. Some might be asking, What is a worldview? Simply stated, a worldview is the framework or set of core beliefs and values by which a person views and interprets reality. You may have heard it said that everyone is a theologian, and everyone has a theology. But the question arises, Is their theology biblically sound or not? The same applies to worldview.

Having a biblical worldview means that our core beliefs and values are informed by the infallible Word of God. God's Word isn't something we just read and study, nor is it something we just hear expounded on Sunday mornings. The Word of God is the foundation for all of life, the lens through which we view the world, enabling us to answer life's hardest questions, such as: Who am I? Where did I come from? Why am I here? Where am I going?

Thank God that our lives can be rooted in the objective, authoritative truth of His Word as we stand amid the howling cultural winds of our own day. So, in seeking to cultivate a biblically sound worldview, we must be rooted and grounded in God's Word, established in the faith, just as we've been taught.

The Trouble with the Church

George Barna has conducted extensive research regarding worldview and the North American church. His findings are deeply troubling. His research has discovered that only nine percent of American Christians possess a biblical worldview.[1] That is not nine percent of Americans; that is nine percent of Americans inside the church. Lacking that filter, most Christians make important decisions based on instinct, emotion, assumptions, past experiences, external pressure, or chance.

What this means is that the majority of Western Christians are walking aimlessly through life with a worldview that is informed by cultural ideologies and worldly philosophies, rather than the Word of God. So, where do we begin to address this very serious problem? God's Word not only has the answer—God's Word *is* the answer. It's the only tried and true foundation for all of faith and life.

Foundations Matter

A firm foundation makes all the difference in the world. Indeed, Jesus spoke to this very issue at the conclusion of His Sermon on the Mount (Matt. 7:24-27). He said that there are two kinds of builders and two kinds of foundations: the wise person who builds a house on the rock and the foolish person who builds a house on sand. When the winds of the

---

1   arizonachristian.edu/wp-content/uploads/2020/04/CRC-AWVI-2020-Release-02_Faith-and-Worldview-1.pdf

world come crashing in, the only house left standing is the one that was built upon the rock. That rock is God's Word, and the wise builder is the person who both hears the Word of God and puts it into practice. That person's house is built on a firm foundation that is immovable.

We're currently living in a time of great upheaval, when the winds of culture are blowing fiercely. Many of us who've experienced this in significant ways are crying out for stability. Perhaps you're crying out from that firm foundation; but for others, perhaps the storms and winds have been so severe that you're becoming disillusioned by life—you're wondering whether a firm foundation is even possible. I want to remind you of Jesus' enduring words, that no matter how bad the storms may be, and no matter how strong the winds may blow—if you've built your house on the rock of God's Word, that firm foundation cannot be shaken. If you've been building your life upon the sinking sand, it's not too late to change. In fact, it's critical for you to do so.

1

Creation

The introduction laid the foundation for establishing a biblical worldview that is rooted and grounded in the Word of God. As a reminder, a worldview is the framework or set of core beliefs and values by which a person views and interprets reality. As we continue, we'll be looking at two primary texts that address the subject of origins (Gen. 1:1-5; John 1:1-5). We begin with the opening chapter of Genesis.

The Creation Account in Genesis 1:1-5

The Bible's opening salvo reveals God's "work" of creating something from nothing, and then shaping that something into the world we now experience.

> In the beginning, God created the heavens and the earth. The earth was without form and void, and darkness was over the face of the deep. And the Spirit of God was hovering over the face of the waters. And God said, "Let there be light," and there was light. And God saw that the light was good. And God separated the light from the darkness. God called the light Day, and the darkness he called Night. And there was evening and there was morning, the first day.

This passage will go on to show that God created the heavens and earth in six days, but on the seventh day He rested, setting it apart as special (Gen. 1:6-2:3). This would have been creation's first Sabbath rest. Later texts reveal that even animals were to participate in the Sabbath established by God at creation (cf. Exod. 20:8-11).

When we think of rest, we shouldn't think that God needed to rest in the same way we do. God's work in creation, rather, serves as the pattern for us to model as we engage in the cultural mandate of Genesis 1:28. We are to conduct our work over a six-day period, and to rest on the seventh day.[1]

Perhaps you think that the idea of God creating the world and everything in it in such a short period of time is difficult to believe. In fact, the same thing could be said about the resurrection—and this is why we need Scripture. We wouldn't know these truths unless God revealed them to us. And this brings us to our second primary text concerning the Bible's teaching on origins.

The Creation Account in John 1:1-5

> In the beginning was the Word. And the Word was with God, and the Word was God. He was in the beginning with God. All things were made through him, and without him was not anything made that was made. In him was life, and the life was the light of men. The light shines in the darkness, and the darkness has not overcome it.

The Gospel of John opens with a prologue introducing us to the very person about whom it was written: Jesus Christ

---

1 These Scriptures testify strongly to the view that understands God's work in creation as having been conducted over a period of six consecutive twenty-four-hour periods, with the seventh day set apart for rest.

(John 1:1-18). And what we learn from these verses is astounding! The opening phrase, "In the beginning," takes us back to Genesis 1:1, where we've already read about God creating the heavens and the earth. But here, John tells us something more. He tells us that there was another person there in that beginning. A person who is called "the Word."

Not only was the Word with God in the beginning—the beginning before the world was created—but the Word was God! Two persons in the presence of one another, both of whom are called "God" (singular), and both of whom were pre-existent before they began their creative work. And we must not forget that there was another person there in that beginning. The Holy Spirit was present, brooding over the deep, ready to bring forth light and life to the world through the eternal Word that was spoken by the Father (Gen. 1:2). Moreover, we discover that everything owes its existence to that eternal Word, which is none other than the second person of the Holy Trinity, the only begotten Son of the Father (John 1:14, 18).[2]

The Conceptual Background for the Word (*Logos*)

The biblical teaching on the Trinity clearly points to the Son as the eternal *Logos* through whom all things were created. Many have sought to wrap their minds around this concept. How can a person be called the *Logos*? What does it mean? What is the background for such a concept? Of the three primary views (Greek philosophy, personified Wisdom,

---

2 The Father, Son, and Holy Spirit are three persons sharing the one divine nature we call "God." For an excellent introduction to the biblical teaching on the Trinity, see Scott R. Swain, *The Trinity: An Introduction*. Short Studies in Systematic Theology. Eds. Graham A. Cole and Oren R. Martin (Wheaton: Crossway, 2020).

and the Word of God in the Old Testament), the strongest evidence points to the Word of God in the Old Testament.

It may be true that the apostle John's choice of the word *Logos* was meant to connect with his Gentile (Greek) hearers/readers. First-century Greco-Romans would have understood this term considering the Greek philosophical thought of the Stoics (c. 336–263 B.C.). Speaking to this, commentator Andreas Köstenberger writes, "In Stoic thought, logos was reason, the impersonal rational principle governing the universe."[3] This *Logos* was later deified in Greek philosophical thought and placed on the same level as the chief god of the Greek pantheon, Zeus.

But for the apostle John and for us as well, Stoic philosophy falls short of the *Logos* revealed to us in Scripture. This *Logos* is not impersonal reason. He's the second person of the Triune God, which is why we need God's special revelation to understand these things. At best, humanity can employ God-given reason to deduce logical truisms from patterns observed through natural revelation, but these observations will never arrive at the fullness of truth. Therefore, if we are to know God as He is, He must reveal Himself to us. And this He has done through the *Logos*, who is a person, the eternally begotten Son of God.

As we consider the various backgrounds for John's use of *Logos*, we're immediately drawn to the Old Testament. The apostle, being of Jewish descent himself, would have been just as concerned to reach his Jewish hearers/readers as he would have been to reach his Gentile audience. This being the case, it's highly likely that the conceptual background for John's *Logos* was not personified Wisdom, but the Word

---

3 Andreas J. Köstenberger, *Encountering John: The Gospel in Historical, Literary, and Theological Perspective*, 2nd ed. (Grand Rapids: Baker, 2013), 40.

of God, first spoken by God and then written down in sacred Scripture. Consider what God has to say through the prophet Isaiah:

> For my thoughts are not your thoughts, neither are your ways my ways, declares the Lord. For as the heavens are higher than the earth, so are my ways higher than your ways and my thoughts than your thoughts. For as the rain and the snow come down from heaven and do not return there but water the earth, making it bring forth and sprout, giving seed to the sower and bread to the eater, so shall *my word be that goes out from my mouth*; it shall not return to me empty, but shall accomplish that which I purpose, and shall succeed in the thing for which I sent it. (Isa. 55:8-11, emphasis mine)

Speaking to this, Köstenberger writes, "while the word of God in Isaiah remains a … [personification] of God's word, John's logos is an actual historical person, the incarnate Lord Jesus Christ."[4] And I would add, He's also the eternal pre-existent Son.

In reflecting on how God has spoken throughout the Old Testament era, what we learn from the apostle John is that God has been speaking to the prophets through His divine Son! And not only this, but as we've seen already, the entire cosmos owes its existence to that same divine Son, who was there in the beginning, and later became one of us in order to accomplish His work of redemption. Consider what the writer to the Hebrews says about these things:

> Long ago, at many times and in many ways, God spoke to our fathers by the prophets, but in these last days *he has spoken to us by his Son*, whom he appointed heir of all things, *through whom also he created the world*. He is the radiance of the glory of God and the exact imprint of his nature, and *he upholds the*

---

4 Köstenberger, *Encountering John*, 43.

universe by the word of his power. After making purification for sins, he sat down at the right hand of Majesty on high… (Heb. 1:1-3, emphasis mine).

As you ponder these things, allow them to sink in deeply. This is the foundational truth concerning reality. The world and everything in it would never have existed apart from the creative work of God through His Son, who is the eternal and incarnate Word of God. And creation would cease to exist if it weren't upheld every moment by that same powerful Word, who is Jesus Christ Himself! Even more, God has not only given us words about Himself to read on a page. In Jesus, God has translated Himself into human nature by becoming a man like us.

Why the Biblical Teaching on Creation Matters

The Bible's teaching on creation matters because it answers some of life's most important questions, especially the questions about origin. Consider the popularity of *Ancestry. com*. It's said that they collect over one billion dollars in revenue annually.[5] Why is this the case? Because people are searching. They want to know where they came from. They want to put all the important pieces of their lives together in order to make sense of who they are. And this search is directly related to the question of origin, the question of where it all began.

The biblical teaching on creation tells us who we are and where we came from. The foundational truth we learn from Genesis 1:1 and its parallel and explanatory passage, John 1:1, is that God is the source of our origin. Therefore, God is absolute reality.

---

5   variety.com/2023/digital/news/amazon-q4-2022-revenue-beats-profit-falls-1235510405/

Note carefully that both biblical texts open with the phrase, "In the beginning…" Some theologians have said that these words are among the most important words of Scripture. If you can believe, "In the beginning, God created the heavens and the earth," you can believe everything else the Bible teaches. If you believe that God existed prior to creation, then everything else will fall into place. The supernatural won't seem strange to you, because the creation itself is a miracle of God!

The truth that God existed before anything came into being affirms that God alone is absolute reality. Thus, there's a distinction between the Creator and the creature. You and I derive our existence from Him. Therefore, He's the one who assigns our identity and purpose. We don't. And that's a good thing. God is not only the absolute reality from which creation derives its existence, He's also the primary character of the Scripture He inspired. In fact, the designation "God" appears thirty-four times in the opening prologue of Genesis (Gen. 1:1-2:3). History is ultimately not about us, it's all about God.

Some may say that it takes great faith to believe that creation was a direct act of God. This may be true. But it takes even greater faith to believe that God doesn't exist and that the universe just suddenly appeared out of non-living matter.[6] First of all, how can living things come from non-living matter? And how can personality come from impersonal matter? It takes greater faith to believe in evolution and spontaneous generation than to believe that the personal Triune God is the source of creation, which includes all living creatures and inanimate objects.

---

6 This is often referred to as *spontaneous generation*.

The Biblical Teaching on Creation Refutes the Lies of Relativism and Autonomy

The truth that God is the source of creation is foundational for confronting the culture's false claims to truth, and here I have two specific falsehoods in mind. The first is the lie of relativism: since there is no absolute being, such as God, there's no absolute truth. The lie of relativism posits that truth is relative. Truth can be whatever you want it to be, so long as we co-exist with one another.

But do you see the problem with the assertion that there's no absolute truth? This assertion itself is a truth claim! As such, its claim is self-contradictory. Not only that, but it's also untenable. No one lives as though there's no absolute truth. And the place this comes to the fore is with the issue of morality.

For example, if someone breaks into your house and steals your valuables, you wouldn't say, "Oh well, that's life. Whoever stole my goods probably thinks that it's okay to take other people's stuff. I guess that's their truth, whoever they may be." No. You would immediately call the police and file a report, because you know that stealing is wrong, and that whoever took your goods should return them or reimburse you for them, as well as face time in jail! Why? Because God does exist, and He has implanted His moral law within our consciences (cf. Rom. 1:18-20), so that even the most ardent unbeliever believes that stealing is wrong. Why? Because God has said, "You shall not steal" (Exod. 20:15) and everyone knows that stealing is wrong, however they may try to justify it.

The truth that God is the source of creation also confronts the lie of autonomy, the quest to live independently of God. In what way? Because it speaks to God's sovereign majesty and power over everything He created. Not only did He speak the created world into existence, but as we've already seen, He continues to uphold it moment by moment through the *Logos*, who is God's eternally begotten Son.

Conversely, our culture wants us to believe in self-sovereignty, but this is not reality. If God is the source of creation, then He is King over all. In fact, Jesus tells us that we have no power to add even a single hour to our lives (Matt. 6:27), let alone avoid death, the great equalizer that comes to all. Moreover, Scripture tells us that every day of our lives has been ordained by God even before we were ever born (Ps. 139:16)—now that's sovereignty!

In essence, the lies of relativism and autonomy posit that you are a god. Think about it: if you can create your own reality, then you are a god. This was the original temptation Adam and Eve succumbed to in the Garden of Eden (Gen. 3:5), and it continues to manifest itself in every generation through some philosophical thought or idea because at the end of the day there's really nothing new under the sun (Eccles. 1:9). The lies of relativism and autonomy are the lies of Genesis 3 all over again.

The fact that God is the absolute reality and is sovereign over His creation is good news because if you or I were sovereign, we would be in big trouble. In fact, when you look at the world and see the mess that human beings have made with the power they do have, can you imagine what the world would be like if they had absolute authority and power in the same way God does? It would be a living nightmare. Be thankful that God is sovereign and we're not. Be thankful that nothing can happen outside of His control. "In the beginning, God ..." is one of the great foundational truths. But there's more.

The Design and Order in Creation

Another thing that testifies to God as the ultimate reality is the design and order we see in creation. Genesis 1:1-2 informs us that God created the heavens and earth "without form and void," and that darkness covered the primordial waters. But as Genesis continues, we begin to see the designer at work.

On days one through three, God goes about the work of separating and forming three main spheres: light and darkness, the heavens and primordial water, the seas and dry land (Gen. 1:3-13). And on days four through six, He fills the newly formed spheres with creatures suitable to their habitats: the heavenly bodies to govern the day and the night, birds to fly above the earth, fish to swarm in the sea, and land animals—with the high point being the creation of humanity in God's image (Gen. 1:14-26)!

The Implications of the Design and Order in Creation

The first thing to observe is that the design and order seen in creation inevitably point to a grand designer. Secondly, the fact that this designer forms and fills His newly created cosmos with creatures suitable to their governing spheres, assigning each its identity and purpose, once again demonstrates that He is the absolute reality, the King of creation, and sovereign Lord over all! Thirdly, the design and order observed in creation give us the basis for conducting modern science. This may be surprising, since we're often told that science is antithetical to the biblical teaching on creation. But this is simply not the case.

In fact, significant scientific discoveries occurred in the Western world during the medieval period, challenging the prevailing views of their time. Scientists such as Nicolaus

Copernicus would never have conducted their research in the first place had they not believed that the creation was good (Gen. 1:31).[7] As one commentator notes, if people believed that matter was evil, they'd be fearful to probe its mysteries.[8] You can observe this fear in animistic cultures, where they believe that nature is alive with spirits. Their concern is not to disturb the spirits, lest they incur their wrath. Indeed, very few people would have embarked upon scientific enterprise had they not believed that creation was good.

But it is also important to recognize that creation was designed and ordered by a rational, purposeful God who had given humanity dominion to explore and develop the world as His vice-regents (Gen. 1:28). God created humanity to grow in understanding of the world, developing the world further each generation. That is, He created us to be scientists! And the scientific method only makes sense if the creation was designed in a rational, orderly fashion. If the world is orderly, you can expect to discover truths about the world from observation and testing. If the world is a random accident, there is no reason to believe that physical laws will function the same in different places or at different times, or that mathematics could produce consistent, accurate results everywhere. If we lived in an accidental world, gravity in Fort Lauderdale might well be completely different in Shanghai— or different in both places tomorrow. If everything appeared randomly without a Creator, there's no reason to believe everything will not disappear a month from now.

---

7   Copernicus was a mathematician and astronomer who proposed that the sun was stationary in the center of the universe and the earth revolved around it as opposed to the geocentric theory that was the reigning view of the day. See plato.stanford.edu/entries/copernicus/.

8   cslewis.org/journal/science-and-christian-faith-conflict-or-cooperation/

Furthermore, if evolution is true, then our ability to think came about through random, accidental chemical processes, without any rational purpose or design. If that's the case, there is no reason to assume that our minds have developed enough to even distinguish truth from delusion; perhaps humanity requires another ten million years of development before we will actually understand the truth. The irony here is that the scientific method, which modern critics claim has disproven God, depends entirely upon the biblical worldview being true. Without the biblical worldview, every assumption of science and rationality is undermined. And this leads to the fourth point: the design and order observed in creation provide the basis for human flourishing.

Let's begin with Genesis 1:27, which reveals that humans are created in God's image and likeness. This doctrine establishes humanity's unique position in creation and defines our essential nature. This divine imprint encompasses both male and female, with God intentionally creating humanity as a complementary duality: "male and female he created them." This teaching reveals that biological sex is not incidental but integral to God's design, woven into the very fabric of human identity. The distinct creation of man and woman reflects God's wisdom in establishing complementary differences that, when properly understood and embraced, lead to human flourishing both individually and in community. Just as a master craftsman designs each component of his work with specific purpose, God has imbued maleness and femaleness with distinct characteristics that, together, reflect different aspects of His nature.

This divine design is not merely superficial but encompasses the totality of human nature—biological, psychological, and spiritual. Contemporary attempts to alter or transcend these created distinctions through medical interventions represent a departure from God's intended design. Such efforts to redefine or reconstruct human nature often result in physical and psychological distress, as they work against rather than with the Creator's blueprint. True fulfillment and wholeness come not from attempting to override these created distinctions but from understanding and embracing our God-given identity as male or female. When we align ourselves with God's design, we experience the harmony and purpose that comes from living in accordance with our created nature.

Next in Genesis 1:28 we read of God's blessing over His human vice-regents as they engage the cultural mandate: "And God blessed them. And God said to them, 'Be fruitful and multiply and fill the earth and subdue it and have dominion over the fish of the sea and over the birds of the heavens and over every living thing that moves on the earth.'" But it's important here to underscore the fact that humanity can only experience life to the fullest if we stay within the bounds of Scripture. The God who gave humanity dominion over the creation is the same God who has also set our boundaries (cf. Gen. 2:16-17), and these boundaries are intended for human flourishing (cf. Deut. 8:1-20).

If we refuse to live under God's authority, we can be assured that our lives will be marked by confusion and will ultimately end in destruction. It's the Devil's lie to believe that we can experience freedom apart from God's authority (cf. Gen. 3:1-19). True freedom exists for those who have followed the call of wisdom, which is the wisdom found in God's Word, and have steered clear of the seductive and deceitful voice of folly (Prov. 8:1–9:18).

Speaking of folly, in 2016, the atheist scientist Graham Lawton wrote an article in *The New Scientist* magazine entitled, "What is the Meaning of Life?" He wrote,

> The harsh answer is "it has none." Your life may feel like a big deal to you, but it's actually a random blip of matter and energy in an uncaring and impersonal universe. When it ends, a few people will remember you for a while, but they will die too. Even if you make the history books, your contribution will soon be forgotten. Humans will go extinct; Earth and the sun will be destroyed. Eventually the universe itself will end. Against this appalling reality, how can a human life have any real meaning?[9]

If what he's saying is true, then there is no God who is absolute reality. There is no truth. There are no moral standards. Nothing is sacred, not even human life. There is no future, and there is no hope. If these things are true and the biblical teaching on creation is wrong, then you don't miss out on anything. But if these things are false—and they are—then you miss out on everything. Think about it very seriously. Are you comfortable dismissing the truth: "In the beginning, God"? If so, then, sadly, you are joining the ranks of folly: "The fool says in his heart, 'There is no God'" (Ps. 14:1). Please don't be a fool.

For those who have rejected God, deep down in your heart you know you're missing something. Every one of us is on a quest for meaning and purpose. We know that there's something beyond ourselves, that there's an answer to life's most challenging questions. And so, here we've come full circle. The biblical teaching on creation tells us where

9 newscientist.com/article/mg23130890-500-metaphysics-special-what-is-the-meaning-of-life/

we came from and who we are. It informs our purpose in life and ultimately points to future hope—the hope that suffering and death are not the final word. There is a God who made everything, a God who is sovereign over all, and a God who will one day finish what He began at creation.

The good news is that this God loves us—and He loves us so much that He sent His Son to save us. And even now, He continues to invite all who will come to Him in faith to turn from folly and live. We close with these fitting words from the apostle Paul:

> [I]f anyone is in Christ, he is a new creation. The old has passed away; behold, the new has come ... Therefore, we are ambassadors for Christ, God making his appeal through us. We implore you on behalf of Christ, be reconciled to God. For our sake he made him to be sin who knew no sin [Jesus Christ], so that in him we might become the righteousness of God. (2 Cor. 5:17, 20-21)

Turn to Jesus and live!

A Prayer of Recognition and Submission

Sovereign Lord and Creator, we stand in awe before your majesty, recognizing that every star, mountain, and breath of life flows from your creative power. You spoke, and the universe leaped into being; you ordained the laws of nature and sustain all things by your mighty Word. We confess that we often live as though we were lords of our own lives, forgetting that we are creatures made by your hands and for your purposes. Forgive our pride and self-will, O God. Help us to embrace our place as your creatures, finding joy and freedom in submitting to your perfect design. May we honor you in how we steward your creation, how we treat our fellow image-bearers, and how we order our lives according to your wisdom rather than our own understanding. Give us humble and teachable hearts that delight in your ways, knowing that as our creator, you alone know what is best for us. We rest in the truth that your authority over us flows from your love, and that in bowing before you as Lord, we find our truest purpose and deepest satisfaction. In the name of Jesus Christ, through whom all things were made, we pray. Amen.

Application Questions

- When you compare Genesis 1 and John 1, it might seem like John is playing fast and loose with the text, or that he is seeing things in Genesis that simply aren't there. Read Luke 24:13-35.

  Jesus tells His disciples that all Scripture, from Moses to the Prophets, reveal Him. In light of this, is John's reading of Genesis arbitrary, or does he grasp a truth we often don't consider? If all Scripture points to Jesus, how might this change how you read the Old Testament? What are some questions you might ask whenever you read the Old Testament in order to notice how it points to Jesus?

- Moral relativism is a worldview that maintains that all truth is subjective—that what may be *your* truth isn't true for everyone else. Why would this be such an attractive idea to many people? How have you found yourself thinking this way in your own life and dealings with people? If everyone acted as if their subjective feelings were the only guide to truth, how would this affect our ability to reason or work together? If moral relativism were adopted, what would that mean for courts and the pursuit of justice in society? How does moral relativism relate to Satan's temptation of Eve—"Did God really say?"

- One core conviction of the biblical worldview is the idea that how something is designed reveals its purpose. Consider a hammer—if you used a hammer as a serving spoon, it would work to a degree, but not well. That's because a hammer was *designed* for the purpose of driving nails, not ladling soup, and everything about its design fits its purpose. Likewise, if you set out to build a house using a large spoon, you won't get very far for the same reason.

  If humanity was created for a purpose and everything about us—our bodies, ability to think and reason, and our purpose—is designed by God, what does that mean for how we should live? If we believe that we are fully autonomous and free to do as we please and pursue whatever desires we have, will we flourish in the same way as if we lived according to our purpose and design? God designed men and women to be different in order that they would fit together. When people reject God's design for their relationships with one another, what effects does this have on society as a whole?

- It is common for Christians today to believe that the sum of the biblical message and the good news is that we get to go to heaven when we die. But this misses most of the biblical story. God didn't just create us to go to a spiritual world after we die, but to *live* in the good world He created in a way that reflects God's character and nature *before* we die, for the sake of His kingdom. God created us to be productive—to be married and have children (be fruitful and multiply), to subdue/cultivate the earth (to productively develop ourselves and the world), and to have dominion (to govern our life and take responsibility for where we live and have influence). Jesus gave us the Great Commission, commanding us to make disciples not only of individuals, but *nations.*

Consider your life currently. Do you believe that what you do on a daily basis (your work, your family life, your hobbies and recreations) has any purpose, or are you just killing time until you get to heaven? What areas in your life are chaotic and need to be brought into order? What sin do you need to repent of and turn away from if you are to become a more mature and faithful person to God and to the purposes He has given you? What changes would you make or new goals would you pursue if you began focusing more on seeking God's purposes for humanity *in this life*?

2

The Sanctity of Human Life

In our last chapter on origins, we addressed the important subject of why the biblical teaching on creation matters. There we discovered that the doctrine of creation tells us who we are and where we came from. It informs our purpose in life and points to future hope—the hope that suffering and death are not the final word.

This chapter builds upon the previous one by unpacking what it means to have a biblical worldview concerning human life. We'll be taking a closer look at Genesis 1:26-27, for there we find the foundational teaching on the image of God in all human life, what theologians have called the *Imago Dei*.

> Then God said, "Let us make man in our image, after our likeness. And let them have dominion over the fish of the sea and over the birds of the heavens and over the livestock and over all the earth and over every creeping thing that creeps on the earth." So, God created man in his own image, in the image of God he created him; male and female he created them.

A Day of Infamy

On December 8, 1941, President Franklin D. Roosevelt stood before Congress after the bombing of Pearl Harbor that left 2,400 dead and declared that it would be "a date that lives in infamy."[1] Indeed, it's infamy was one of darkness and destruction. Likewise, January 22, 1973, will be a day that lives in infamy because on that day the United States Supreme Court legalized abortion on demand in every state. Thankfully, this decision was reversed in 2022 and authority was passed back to the states. Unfortunately, there are many state legislatures that will continue to uphold the so-called woman's right to choose. Even worse, there are many so-called Christians who hold to a pro-choice position. This is a fatal flaw of the modern church not being grounded with a biblical worldview concerning human life. How should the people of God respond? We need to go back to the Word of God to inform our response concerning this cultural moment and this attack on the sanctity of human life.

The Sanctity of All Human Life

Christians have historically affirmed that all human life, from the moment of fertilization, has intrinsic value because we are made in the image of God (Gen. 1:26-27).

The first foundational truth we learn from Genesis 1:26-27 is that all human life is sacred. These verses reveal that there's something unique about humanity that sets it apart from the rest of creation and all other created beings. This foundational truth is the fact that human beings are made in God's image and, therefore, all human life is precious in His sight. Do you understand the significance of this?

---

1 Speech by Franklin D. Roosevelt, address to Congress, December 8, 1941.

The message of Genesis 1:26 is that God creates us in His image so that we will be like Him. Think about that! God desires for us to never forget that we are sacred and created with a moral compass to reflect the one who created the heavens and the earth. This very truth is what separates us from all other creatures. This is what makes all human life sacred without exception. It also means that our worth is found in who we *are* and not in what we *do*.

If human life were only valuable because of what someone can *do*, this would mean that certain lives are worthless. If so, it becomes easy to justify eliminating people who fall into purportedly less valuable categories. But if all human beings are God's image, then all people are *intrinsically* valuable—regardless of their worldview, ethnicity, social status, mental capacity, age, or any other categorization. The doctrine of the image of God is the great equalizer that makes every person equal and valuable in His sight.

Moreover, what's amazing to me is that this truth of the image of God in all human beings is ingrained in each one of us—so ingrained that we know it's true. For example, perhaps you've found yourself watching *Animal Planet* or other shows that have gazelles running through the fields, and out of nowhere comes a pride of lions that tears them to pieces. No one that I'm aware of ever calls *Animal Planet* and says, "This is an atrocity! You must take down this show immediately." But if you were walking down the street and saw an individual take another person's life, you would cry out in outrage. Why? Because deep within, we all know that there's something sacred that distinguishes human beings from the rest of creation. It's the doctrine of the image of God in humanity that makes all human life sacred, and this is without exception. But there's more.

The Beginning and End of Human Life

The second foundational truth is this: the reality that human life begins at fertilization. This is so important. Since Genesis is the foundational text for understanding the sanctity of human life, from this we can also infer something about when human life begins. And this is critical, because although you may believe everything that you've read so far and you would agree that all human life is sacred, you may still ask, when does human life begin? Genesis 1:26-27 tells us that God is the author of human life. And while it's true that our first parents were created as the direct act of God (Gen. 2:7, 21), nevertheless, He created and blessed them with the powers of procreation to produce children that would bear His divine image (Gen. 1:28).[2] As such, the continuing creative power of God takes place inside a mother's womb.

You may be familiar with Psalm 139:13: "For you formed my inward parts. You knitted me together in my mother's womb." In this text, God is speaking about personhood being established from the moment of conception. Personhood doesn't begin once a baby is born, nor does it begin when a child develops the faculty of reason. A baby is a person from the moment of conception. But here's the problem. The motto of our culture is, "My body, my choice." It's one of the most absurd things I've ever heard. If it's true that all human life is sacred, and personhood begins in the womb, then that person inside of a woman's body is a separate entity. There is another *person*, with a distinct body, living inside the body of his or her mother. Therefore, abortion cannot be "her body, her choice."

---

2 After the fall of humanity, recorded in Genesis 3, we still retain the image of God, even though it's a broken image (cf. Gen. 5:3; 9:6).

Still others might say that science disagrees. Oh, really? We've already established through Scripture that personhood begins at fertilization. And for all those skeptics who say that science contradicts Scripture, I invite them to think again. From the moment of fertilization, two sets of DNA merge within the egg, producing a unique genetic structure, which never has or ever will exist again. From that moment, a new human life has formed and begins to develop *on its own*. Technological developments from science have demonstrated that at eight weeks of age, the baby in the womb can suck its thumb. He or she can feel pain and respond to sound. The brain is active. The heart is pumping. The kidneys are producing cleansing fluid throughout the baby's body. And we know that at twenty-one weeks of age a baby can survive outside its mother's womb. It's the Word of God (special revelation) and technological discoveries within the medical field (general revelation) that tell us that this baby is another body existing inside its mother's womb.[3]

The reality that a baby is a person from the moment of conception affirms this foundational truth: we cannot kill babies—period! The pro-choice movement is nothing more than demonic propaganda wrapped in the virtue of personal liberty, and we, as the people of God, need to stand up and proclaim the truth regarding the sanctity of all human life. These two truths give us a biblical foundation for human life.

Furthermore, just as we must affirm the sanctity of human life at its beginning, we must equally defend it at its

---

3   See this article on Bernard Nathanson's film, The Silent Scream. embryo.asu.edu/pages/silent-scream-1984-bernard-nathanson-crusade-life-and-american-portrait-films. Dr. Nathanson was an abortionist who changed his views with the invention of ultrasound in which he was able to view a baby inside its mother's womb.

end. The growing acceptance of euthanasia and physician-assisted suicide represents another assault on the image of God in humanity. When we declare that some lives are not worth living due to illness, age, or disability, we usurp God's authority as the author of life and death. The same Scripture that teaches us about God's creative work in the womb also shows us that our days are numbered by Him (Ps. 139:16). Even in suffering, human life retains its God-given dignity and worth. To intentionally end a life, whether through euthanasia or assisted suicide, is to reject God's sovereignty and wisdom in determining the length of our days. While we should absolutely pursue excellent palliative care and support for those facing terminal illness, we must reject the false compassion that sees death as a solution to suffering.

The Priority of the Unborn and the Elderly

Many have criticized the pro-life movement for solely focusing on the issue of abortion. Let me first say that Christians must be concerned for all human life, from womb to the tomb. We are called to defend the marginalized and vulnerable of society. The question is, who is the most vulnerable? The unborn—those who literally have no capacity to defend themselves. If we do not prioritize defending human life in the womb, we have no hope in defending human life outside of the womb. Biblical justice for all people begins with the unborn.

Similarly, we must recognize that our elderly and terminally ill brothers and sisters are increasingly vulnerable to the culture of death through euthanasia and assisted suicide. Just as we fight for the unborn, we must defend those at the end of life who face pressure to "die with dignity"—a euphemism that masks the tragic reality of premature death. The same worldview that devalues life in the womb also seeks to eliminate those deemed too burdensome or costly to care for. When a society begins to measure human worth by utility rather than dignity, it inevitably creates categories of lives "unworthy of life." As Christians, we must demonstrate that true dignity comes not from autonomy or capability, but from being created in God's image—an identity that persists through every stage of life, including its final chapter.

So how should we respond? What follows are some practical suggestions.

The Response of God's People

The first thing we can do is to get involved in the effort to promote the sanctity of human life. There's really no excuse not to. Whether you're a teenager or a senior adult, you can and should get involved. There are numerous opportunities available. You can give, you can serve, you can fill out a petition, you can vote, and you can pray. Why is this so important? Because, for far too long, many of God's people have shaken their fists at the darkness but done nothing about it. We may complain about the pro-choice movement, but until we become more fully engaged, our words are rather empty. So, take a stand. Not tomorrow, but today—and respond. Be a beacon of hope and light amid the darkness. Here are two helpful encouragements: first, know the facts, and second, get involved.

It's amazing to see how many people are ignorant of the statistics, which is a large part of the problem. Did you know that over sixty million babies have been aborted since *Roe v. Wade*?[4] Did you know that 92 percent of Down syndrome

---

4 foxnews.com/politics/abortions-since-roe-v-wade

babies in America are aborted? Ninety-two percent of Down syndrome babies are aborted because their mother and father say they aren't wanted in society.[5] The numbers are worse in Iceland where Down syndrome has been reduced by 99 percent through abortion.[6] We heard a lot about the pandemic in 2020. In that year, 1.8 million people lost their lives to COVID.[7] Do you know how many babies around the world lose their lives to abortion each year? According to the World Health Organization, 73 million.[8] That, my friends, is a global pandemic. Be informed. Know the facts. And do something about it.

Lastly and just as important, be a people who offer the hope that's in Jesus Christ—the hope and forgiveness that are found in His cross work alone. If the statistics are true, six out of ten (61 percent) women with unplanned pregnancies and three out of ten (29 percent) of all pregnancies end in abortion.

This means that there's a strong possibility that someone you know has either had an abortion or may be presently contemplating one. Please hear me on this: no one is ever beyond the grace and mercy of Jesus. As a pastor of Christ's church, I want everyone to know that there's hope and forgiveness. The message of the gospel is this: there is restoration in Jesus Christ alone. We need to be faithful in calling everyone to repent, believe, and be saved. Maybe you're a woman contemplating abortion. Would you reach

---

5 bpas.org/get-involved/campaigns/briefings/fetal-anomaly/

6 cbsnews.com/news/down-syndrome-iceland/

7 academic.oup.com/ije/article/51/1/63/6375510

8 who.int/news-room/fact-sheets/detail/abortion. These statistics appear on the website of an organization that advocates for abortion, a position we strongly disagree with, as this chapter shows.

out to a local pastor, counselor, or pregnancy center? There is real hope for you, regardless of your circumstances.

I close with a story about Joan Andrews, a devout Roman Catholic who was arrested and prosecuted in 1986. Her crime? She conducted peaceful sit-ins at abortion clinics across Florida. The prosecutor suggested one year in prison, but the judge gave her five, just to make a statement. She was asked, "Why would someone risk prison for such a cause?" Her courage came from a childhood incident. When Joan was twelve, her cousin fell into a river and was being swept away. Joan became overwhelmed by fear because she couldn't swim. Recalling the incident she said, "I thought if I tried to save her, we would both drown. But then a greater fear grabbed me, the fear of doing nothing."[9]

People of God, in the face of the monstrous evil of abortion, are you going to sit there and do nothing? Or will the fear of doing nothing grip you to say, "Yes, I will stand in the gap. Yes, I will carry the flag"? Is there another group more persecuted, is there a group that is more vulnerable than that of the unborn? Knowing this, how will you answer the call to advocate for the least of these? May you be motivated by the good news of Jesus Christ, gripped by the fear of doing nothing, and say, "Yes, today is the day that I will answer the call to carry the flag and bring life into this culture of death." And may it be so.

A Prayer of Repentance and Restoration

Our Father and our God, we mourn the sixty plus million babies whose lives have been taken in our

---

9 Charles Colson, "The Fear of Doing Nothing," *Christianity Today*, May 15, 1987.

nation. But, as Christ's church, we offer hope for the world. We are the salt and light of the earth, and we offer the message of forgiveness and hope. And so, may the radical message of the gospel of Jesus Christ so grip the church here in America that one day, for our children and grandchildren, abortion will not only be illegal but unthinkable.

Father, for those who are carrying the heavy weight of the sin and shame of previous decisions, may they know that the gospel declares that they no longer need to wear a scarlet letter, they no longer need to carry the burden of previous sins. There is complete forgiveness for all who come to Him in repentance and faith. May they know His mercy and trust in His forgiveness to begin life anew. May they understand that it's in Jesus alone that they may become a new creation—the old has gone, the new has come. May there be hundreds of testimonies of men and women who receive the full forgiveness of Jesus Christ, who receive His good news and are freed from the heavy weight of sin. And may we, the people of God, be moved to be bearers of truth, taking light into the darkness of our world, promoting a culture of love and life, and advancing your Kingdom, Father, on earth as it is in heaven. In Jesus' name, I pray. Amen.

Application Questions

- Justifying abortion relies on the belief that an unborn child is not really human or should not be considered a person until very late in pregnancy— or even until after that child is born. Some will say, "It's just a fetus" or "a clump of cells." What are some of the ways that this reasoning is flawed?

If someone says an unborn baby is not really a human, how might you respond? Fetus is the Latin word for baby. How might this fact help to turn the conversation when someone dismisses a child as "just a fetus"?

- Consider Psalm 139:13-15:

    For you formed my inward parts;
    you knitted me together in my mother's womb.
    I praise you, for I am fearfully and wonderfully made.
    Wonderful are your works;
    my soul knows it very well.
    My frame was not hidden from you,
    when I was being made in secret,
    intricately woven ...

    Dissect this passage. What is God's relationship with unborn children? In what way is God involved in the process? What should be our response, thinking about how God formed us?

- Consider the previous chapter. In what way does abortion relate to evolution? How does abortion relate to the idea that morality is relative? How does it relate to the idea that humans are autonomous from God? If abortion is the intentional killing of the image of God, what attitude does abortion display toward God?

- God's commission to all humanity in Genesis 1 includes being fruitful, multiplying and filling the earth, and subduing/cultivating it. That is, God intends humanity to grow until the world is filled with His image and intends that the process of cultivating the earth will occur across many generations. In light of this specific task, how does abortion relate to God's purpose for humanity? Is having an abortion a choice without moral consequences, or is it something much more serious?

- Just as it is common to hear pro-abortion arguments that argue based upon the age of the unborn child, it is common to hear arguments in favor of abortion that argue that humans only become valuable once they reach a certain stage ("it's just a fetus"), mental capacity ("this baby would be born with Down syndrome"), etc.

  If we say humans are only valuable in certain circumstances to justify abortion, how might this same reasoning be used in other circumstances? What are some examples of history you can think of that argued for killing or enslaving people based on the concept that they weren't really human, or somehow less than others? How does the doctrine of the image of God keep us from making these errors?

- Abortion is often justified on the basis that a "woman has the right to choose what to do with her body." In what way is this argument based on a false premise? When an abortion occurs, are we only dealing with the *woman's* body? And what about other choices—would it also be morally acceptable for a pregnant woman to use hard drugs while pregnant? Does the Bible teach that we have a right to do whatever we want?

3

The Sovereignty of God

The biblical teaching on God's sovereignty is one of the most foundational and practical truths for the Christian life because it affects everything. Whether you realize it or not, God's sovereignty impacts your family, your vocation, your health, your wealth, what's happening on the world scene—everything! If it weren't for the comfort of knowing that God is sovereign, life would be dismal; I doubt very much I would want to get up in the morning, let alone pursue my life's calling as a pastor. It's this truth that keeps us on stable ground and hopeful about the future. It's the truth that God is sovereign over everything, and He is working all things together for the good of those who love Him, according to His redemptive purposes in Christ.

In this chapter, we'll be looking at the sovereignty of God based upon the apostle Paul's teaching in Romans 8:28-30, 38-39:

> And we know that for those who love God all things work together for good, for those who are called according to his purpose. For those whom he foreknew he also predestined to

be conformed to the image of his Son, in order that he might be the firstborn among many brothers. And those whom he predestined he also called, and those whom he called he also justified, and those whom he justified he also glorified… For I am sure that neither death nor life, nor angels nor rulers, nor things present nor things to come, nor powers, nor height nor depth, nor anything else in all creation, will be able to separate us from the love of God in Christ Jesus our Lord.

God Is in Charge

The first thing the biblical doctrine of sovereignty teaches us is that God is in charge. It reveals that He is the King over His good creation. In fact, the New Testament witnesses to the fact that God has established His Son, Jesus Christ, to be the ruler of the kings of the earth (Ps. 2:2). As such, the earth's rulers are warned to come under His authority lest He become angry, and they perish in the way (Ps. 2:10-12). Jesus doesn't have to ask permission from them to execute His justice and righteousness in the earth. He's in charge and for this reason, the apostle can say with confidence that God is working all things together for good (Rom. 8:28).

God's Sovereignty and Our Sanctification

Now some may be thinking, "I can't see very much that's good in my life right now. How can this Scripture be true?" Well, if you'll look more closely at the text, you'll note that Romans 8:28 doesn't say that "all things are good," but rather that "for those who love God all things work together for good." You see the difference? It's not that everything that comes into our lives is necessarily "good" in and of itself, but rather, God Himself is good and He promises to work everything out for our greater good—with the goal of making us more like His Son, Jesus (Rom. 8:29)! This is called sanctification, and the process of sanctification is oftentimes painful. Yet, unlike many who resist life's more challenging trials, our heavenly Father loves us enough to let us go through the refiner's fire.

The Practical Implications of God's Sovereignty

Practically speaking, this means that every day we wake up, we can rest in the knowledge that God is in charge and that our lives are not in our own hands. They're in the hands of a loving Father (cf. John 10:27-30). Such knowledge should lead us to worship. So let me ask you, do you spend time with God every morning before you start the day? Do you honor and worship Him for who He is, the sovereign, loving, and good God? It would be difficult to honor a God who wasn't in control of things. But the reality is, God is in control and He's good and, thus, worthy of our deepest praise.

The knowledge that God is sovereign over everything not only leads us to rest and worship, but it also fills our hearts with confidence. This means that we don't need to be anxious. Whether we know it or not, many of us are experts at fear and worry. You may be the type of person who's always thinking that something bad is going to happen. But you can be relieved of this anxiety by believing and trusting in the God who is sovereign over everything. Belief in the sovereign God will free you from the "what if…" syndrome. For example, what if the stock market crashes? What if the storm hits? What if I don't get into that college? What if, what if, what if …? As if it's all about us. Remember, God's in charge, and we're not! That's good news. So, let's start living in accordance with this reality.

And here I have a confession to make. Sometimes I lie awake at night and ask myself: "How am I going to lead this church? I'm responsible for the souls of so many people." But then I'm reminded of the promise of my Savior, "I will build *My* church" (Matt. 16:18).

God Is the Author and Finisher of Our Salvation

The reality that God is sovereign over everything also teaches us that He is the Author and Finisher of our salvation. Observe the following:

> For those whom he *foreknew* he also predestined to be conformed to the image of his Son, in order that he might be the firstborn among many brethren. And those whom he *predestined* he also *called*, and those whom he called he also justified, and those whom he justified he also *glorified.* (Rom. 8:29-30; emphasis mine)

You will note that the apostle Paul uses the word *foreknew*. You might say, "This doesn't mean that God chooses to save some and not others. The foreknowledge of God simply means that God looks down the corridor of time and knows those who will choose Him and those who will not. And it's on this basis that He predestines them to salvation in Christ." But that's not the biblical definition of foreknowledge.

Biblical foreknowledge assumes a personal, intimate relationship that originates in God Himself,[1] not in us or any choice we might make. It isn't that God knew about us—foreknowledge here means to love in advance. In His electing love, He predestines men, women, and children to eternal salvation in His Son, Jesus Christ. We learn from this that God does the choosing—we don't. This means that there is absolutely nothing we can do with respect to choosing

---

1 Verlyn D. Verbrugge, "Pronoeō," *New International Dictionary of New Testament Theology* (Grand Rapids: Zondervan, 2003), 491.

or losing our salvation. If we've been chosen in Christ from before the foundation of the world, we will be saved! Thus, God is the Author and Finisher of our salvation—from beginning to end (cf. Eph. 1:3-14).

Now someone might say, "But Pastor, I remember the day that I chose God." Yes, at some point in history, true believers will respond to God's call. However, this is different from our choosing Him. The reality is that if we look back on our experience, we'll observe that it was God who opened our hearts to believe His gospel. Our ability to respond to His call was because He had already chosen us in Christ from before the world began (1 Pet. 1:2). And this truth may be further substantiated by observing Paul's use of the past tense for the verbs that concern our very salvation: those whom God *predestined* He also *called*, the called, He also *justified*, and the justified He also *glorified*. Note well: even our glorification, which is still a future reality, is spoken of in the past tense as though it's a done deal (Rom. 8:30)! From beginning to end, therefore, salvation is the work of God. What a relief this is!

The Practical Implications of God's Sovereignty in Salvation

Embracing the fact that God is the Author and Finisher of salvation should give every true believer an assurance that leads to greater reverence and appreciation for all that He's done and is doing for us. It also serves as a great motivation for evangelism, which may sound strange to some.

Have you heard it said that "if God is sovereign, then why evangelize?" That logic doesn't hold up. If God is sovereign in the work of salvation, then we should have even more confidence to evangelize. God uses the means of evangelism to bring people to saving faith. Scripture says that faith comes by hearing the preached Word. So, how will someone come to faith unless the gospel is preached to them (Rom. 10:14-17)? Indeed, the conviction that God is sovereign in the work of salvation through the proclamation of the gospel is what motivated Dr. D. James Kennedy to launch one of the largest, most successful evangelism ministries in the world—Evangelism Explosion! And it continues to make its impact across the globe today.

And lastly, the reality of God's sovereignty in salvation tells us that He is for us, not against us (Rom. 8:31). How do we know—especially during times when we don't feel His nearness? Look to the cross, the objective evidence of God's love for you and me:

> He who did not spare his own Son but gave him up for us all, how will he not also with him graciously give us all things (Rom. 8:32)?

This is profound. And don't forget that God handed Jesus over while we were still His enemies:

> God shows his love for us in that while we were still sinners, Christ died for us. Since, therefore, we have now been justified by his blood, much more shall we be saved by him from the wrath of God. For if while we were enemies we were reconciled to God by the death of his Son, much more, now that we are reconciled, shall we be saved by his life. More than that, we also rejoice in God through our Lord Jesus Christ, through whom we have now received reconciliation (Rom 5:8-11).

If God did this for us while we were His enemies, will He not then freely give us everything else that He promises through His Word? Yes, God is for us. And if He is for us, who can be against us? No one. And nothing—not even death—will ever be able to separate us from His love for us in Christ Jesus, our Lord (Rom. 8:31-39).

Our God: The Sovereignly Good and Faithful Father

U.S. Army First Lieutenant Todd Weaver was killed by an IED in September 2010, on his second tour of duty in Afghanistan. His wife, Emma, received his belongings shortly after his funeral and burial at Arlington National Cemetery. When she looked through the documents on Todd's laptop computer, she found a letter he had written to her if he was killed in war. And this is what the letter said:

Dear Emma,

Well, if you're reading this, I guess I didn't make it home. And, therefore, I was not able to remind you again of how much I love you. I want you to know just how important you are to me. I could not ask for a more caring, beautiful, loving wife. The memories that we have shared over the last few years have been the best of my life. Although it might seem like my life was cut short, I lived a life that most can only dream of. I married the perfect woman, had a beautiful daughter that amazed me every day. Remind her about her daddy and tell her that I loved her more than anything else in the world. Her birth was the best day of my life. She was the best thing that ever happened to me. Tell her that Daddy is in heaven now. And never forget that God knew what was best for us before we were ever born. Take comfort in that, Emma. My death happened for a reason and, although you might not understand it now, I pray that you will one day. And, although you might think it impossible right now, have faith. Much better times are coming. You and Kylie have a wonderful life ahead, and I am so happy to have shared some of it with you.[2]

---

2   dailymail.co.uk/news/article-1393166/Soldiers-messages-love-baby-

On your worst day, it's the sovereignty of God that grounds us, so that our weary souls don't lose sight of the fact that He's in charge and is sovereign over everything. It's my prayer that these truths become so implanted in our hearts that regardless of the trials in this life, you and I will be immoveable, rooted and grounded in the foundational truths that God is a sovereign, good, and faithful Father and He is working everything together for our good according to His purposes.

A Prayer of Surrender and Trust

Our Father and our God, there may be some who are reading this who've lived their lives according to the creed of autonomy: "I am seeking the self-governed, self-directed life." That's an impossible life to live. I pray that they will surrender their lives to you, Father, the one who is perfectly sovereign and perfectly good. And how are they to know these things about you? Because you did not spare your own Son—you gave Him up for us, for those who hear your call and come. I pray that they come to the end of themselves, realizing that they cannot save themselves. I ask that you convict them of their need to repent of their sins, to change their ways of thinking and living, and to look to Jesus, the one who died and rose for us. May they fall into your sovereign arms, dear Father, knowing that you're in charge, that you are good, and you are always faithful. May they live with the assurance that there is nothing and no one who will ever be able to separate them from your love in Christ Jesus our Lord.

---

daughter-widow-grave-dies-Afghanistan.html

And for those who know you but are going through a very dark season of life, perhaps filled with doubt, anxiety, and fear, may they know, Father, that you are sovereign and good, and that you will work everything out in their lives for the good, after the pattern of your beloved Son. May we all become godly men and women who evaluate the circumstances of our lives through the lens of faith, knowing that you're in charge and you'll be faithful to the end, according to every promise of your Word. In Jesus' name, our Lord and our King. Amen.

Application Questions

- The doctrine of God's sovereignty is uniquely difficult for modern people. But let's not forget *who* we're talking about: "God shows his love for us in this: while we were yet sinners, Christ died for us… [W]hile we were enemies we were reconciled to God by the death of his Son" (Rom. 5:8, 10). Jesus is the perfect revelation of who God is, and God's great love has been shown to us through Christ's willingness to die to redeem us.

  When you think about God's sovereignty, what are your greatest challenges? How does thinking about who *Jesus* is help to deal with those challenges? Scripture says that Jesus endured His suffering on the cross "for the joy that was set before him"—you being saved, forgiven, and made new (Heb. 12:2). Even if you struggle with the idea that God is in control, do you think you can trust Jesus, knowing that He joyfully laid down His life so that you could be redeemed?

- One reason we have such a great difficulty embracing the doctrine of God's sovereignty is that we have a much higher opinion of ourselves than we ought to. That is, we don't really grasp how bad the problem is, often thinking of ourselves as mostly good people who have made some mistakes. Read Genesis 6:5, Romans 8:7, and Ephesians 2:1-10.

  Do these passages say that human beings are naturally good, neutral, or evil? Do we have the ability—or even the desire—to seek God on our own? If, as Ephesians 2 says, we are by nature children of wrath and dead in our sin, how does Paul say that we are saved? Is our salvation a result of something we do or choose, or God?

- Some of you are probably thinking, "Wait, if this is true, then how could God possibly condemn anyone? Wouldn't that be unfair?" It's a reasonable question. But let's think about the idea of our *nature*. Jesus uses the example of healthy trees and diseased trees to describe people. He says, "[N]o good tree produces bad fruit, nor [does] a bad tree produce good fruit" (Luke 6:43).

  Is an apple tree *forced* against its will to produce apples or does it produce apples because it *is* an apple tree? Is a wolf *forced* to eat meat or does it eat meat because it *is* a carnivore? If we are sinners *by nature*, are we *forced* to do evil or is doing evil what we do because of who we *are*? If all our sin is something that arises out of our own hearts and desires, would God be unjust for condemning that evil?

- Romans 8 has been called the "golden chain" of salvation. Those whom God foreknew (loved beforehand) He predestined, called, justified (made righteous), and glorified. I've heard it said that on that golden chain of salvation there is not one human fingerprint—it's all God's work.

  Many find themselves terrified, thinking that God could not love them, or that He could not possibly forgive them for the terrible things they have done. But if our salvation is the result of God's unadulterated mercy, should we have any doubt that God can and will save us if we repent and trust in Christ? If God the Father has chosen to save you, God the Son has shed His blood on the cross to save you, and God the Holy Spirit has made you alive so that you would receive Jesus by faith, is there anything that could keep you from being saved? Is your sin more powerful than the blood of Jesus or the power of God?

- Study after study shows that we are more depressed, anxious, and fearful than ever before. How does the doctrine of God's sovereignty help to alleviate these problems? If you really trusted what God has revealed—everything that happens to you is ultimately going to make you more like Jesus and it all will work out for your good (Rom. 8:28-29)—how would that change those sorts of feelings? If you started acting like God was in charge and that you had nothing to fear, how would that change how you approach your life, your work, your family life, your future?

- One feature of the lives of the apostles and the early church was a kind of fearlessness in the face of death. Read Acts 4:24-31. Many assume that the doctrine of God's sovereignty would lead Christians to abandon evangelism or to think that nothing they do makes a difference. But how does that compare with the early Christians' attitude, prayer, and actions? Did the sovereignty of God weaken or embolden them?

  If you were talking with an unbelieving friend and you believed that their salvation ultimately depended upon your ability to get through to them, wouldn't that pressure—"If I don't say the right things, they could be lost forever"—encourage you to shrink away from having those conversations? On the other hand, if you understood that their salvation is dependent upon the Holy Spirit opening their eyes and you are simply the mouthpiece God has chosen to use to deliver that message, isn't there every reason to be confident and bold?

- In light of what you have learned, consider your own life. In a world with sin, we are all guilty of committing evil, we all face evil, and suffering is inevitable. What are the ways you have experienced God moving to rescue you? What trials has He brought your way and gotten you through?

  Psalm 56:8 says that God keeps a count of how many times we toss and turn in the night, and He collects our tears in a bottle. Our suffering is real. Evil really is evil. Death is a devastating force and our enemy. But God is not calloused toward any of us. If God truly knows you in this way—keeping watch over you on every sleepless night—and intends to work all things for your good, how might this change your perspective from despair to joyful endurance?

4

Absolute Truth

If truth is *absolute,* that means it is true at all times and in all places. This means that truth is unchanging regardless of one's historical situation or their culture's latest philosophical speculations. Let me begin by saying that absolute truth is the norm that not only establishes the way we think, but also informs how we live. Thus, in addressing this important subject, we'll be looking at a passage from 1 John, a letter written to Christians living in Asia Minor during the first century.[1] In this letter, John writes to address two basic concerns. The first, to expose false teachers among them (1 John 2:26), and second, to give true believers assurance of their salvation in Christ (5:13). Let's look at 1 John 2:18-27:

> Children, it is the last hour, and as you have heard that antichrist is coming, so now many antichrists have come. Therefore we know that it is the last hour. They went out

---

1 The author of this letter is John, the apostle. He was one of Jesus' twelve disciples and therefore an eyewitness to the one who is Truth. In addition to the Gospel that bears his name, John is also the author of the Book of Revelation.

from us, but they were not of us; for if they had been of us, they would have continued with us. But they went out, that it might become plain that they all are not of us. But you have been anointed by the Holy One, and you all have knowledge. I write to you, not because you do not know the truth, but because you know it, and because no lie is of the truth. Who is the liar but he who denies that Jesus is the Christ? This is the antichrist, he who denies the Father and the Son. No one who denies the Son has the Father. Whoever confesses the Son has the Father also. Let what you heard from the beginning abide in you. If what you heard from the beginning abides in you, then you too will abide in the Son and in the Father. And this is the promise that he made to us—eternal life. I write these things to you about those who are trying to deceive you. But the anointing that you received from him abides in you, and you have no need that anyone should teach you. But as his anointing teaches you about everything, and is true, and is no lie—just as it has taught you, abide in him.

There are three important emphases that stand out in the above text: the reality of absolute truth, the suppression of absolute truth, and the perseverance of absolute truth. Let's look at each one.

The Reality of Absolute Truth

It's no surprise that we're living in a time of rapid change in the world. Things are moving at such a fast pace that it leaves many wondering if we can count on anything being true. If it's considered true today, will it still be true tomorrow? This Western cultural moment says what's true for you doesn't have to be true for me; we can coexist in alternative realities in which polar "truths" exist, allegedly both being true at the same time. After all, truth is relative, we're told. But Jesus begs to differ. In fact, He is Truth incarnate

(John 14:6). Therefore, His Word is eternal and unchanging truth because Jesus is the eternal, unchanging Son of God (cf. John 1:1-2; Heb. 13:8).

Indeed, the apostle John highlights this when he says, "I write to you, not because you do not know the truth, but because you know it, and because no lie is of the truth" (1 John 2:21). Notice what he doesn't say. John doesn't say that truth is in the eye of the beholder. He doesn't say that truth is up to his audience to define. John says that truth is not dependent upon you. We don't define truth, we simply receive truth through divine revelation.

The Bible teaches that absolute truth exists outside of ourselves. In other words, the truth is no less true whether we choose to believe it or not. Moreover, the Bible teaches that truth doesn't conform to our standards. In fact, it's the reverse. We're called to conform to its standards, or else pay a very heavy price by rejecting it. Let me give you an illustration.

Suppose you're sitting in an airplane that's flying in midair. You've heard about the law of gravity but have decided that it doesn't conform to what you want to believe. You've decided that you'd like to fly on your own. So, you open the emergency side door, and guess what happens? There are some very serious consequences. Realistically speaking, none of us believes that truth is relative. You will observe this especially when it comes to things such as gravity. Reality is what it is, whether we like it or not. To claim that "truth is relative" reveals a deep spiritual and moral problem. It reveals a person's estrangement from God.

So, John writes this letter to implore God's people to hang on to the absolute truth, the truth that has been revealed to them in the person and work of His Son, Jesus Christ. And the same good Word applies to us today. Hold on to the truth amid a culture that has rejected Jesus Christ, who alone is the Way, the Truth, and the Life (John 14:8). For two thousand years, Christians have stood by this claim. The reality of this claim is based upon the eyewitness testimonies of Jesus' disciples who affirm the truth that Jesus is the Christ, the Son of the living God (John 21:31). And if Jesus is the Son of God, which He is, then He is God. Thus, we arrive at no higher absolute than this.

Some may be thinking, "What's the big deal about absolute truth? Can't we just coexist in a society without claiming absolutes?" Have you looked at countries such as the Soviet Union and China that make the claim that God doesn't exist, countries in which 150 million people were murdered under atheistic regimes in the twentieth century alone?[2] This is what happens when you deny the existence of God, the God who is the absolute definer of truth. By denying God we're left with an ethical system that is driven by a godless amoral class of elites who do not care for the least of these, and whose major concern is their own "will to power."[3] The Christian worldview alone provides the true paradigm for reality, the way things *ought* to be believed and obeyed.

Indeed, without truth, which we derive from God, there would be no objective morality and no standard for justice. There would be no love or forgiveness—just slavery and servitude to those who hold power. All the things that we take for granted and hold dear to our hearts—the freedom to create, to live, to laugh, to see our children grow up—

2 premierchristianity.com/home/5-uncomfortable-facts-atheists-need-to-hear/2415.article

3 plato.stanford.edu/entries/nietzsche/

would unravel before our very eyes in a culture that decries, "God is dead." The very living God who is the Absolute is the God from which absolute truth derives. This is the truth that will set us free from the tyranny of the demonic lies of our world. And this leads to our second consideration.

The Suppression of Absolute Truth

In addition to the reality of absolute truth, we see also its suppression. This comes to the fore in 1 John 2:22. Some may find John's language a bit extreme, especially when he says that those who deny the truth are "liars." The modern tendency is to refer to people who deny God's existence simply as having "a difference of opinion," ironically, as though truth were relative. We've become much more accommodating and sometimes even compromising, and this is to our shame. But John calls it for what it is. He calls those who deny the truth about Jesus Christ "liars."

We need to understand what's going on here. What is a liar? A liar is someone who knows the truth but suppresses it; not only do they suppress it, but they also replace it with something else. Therefore, John doesn't give these deniers a pass. He doesn't say they're simply ignorant and uninformed. He doesn't let them off the hook. In fact, there's a parallel passage in Paul's letter to the Romans that helps us understand the real issue. Paul writes,

> For the wrath of God is revealed from heaven against all ungodliness and unrighteousness of men, who by their unrighteousness suppress the truth. For what can be known about God is plain to them, because God has shown it to them. For although they knew God, they did not honor him as God or give thanks to him, but they became futile in their thinking, and their foolish hearts were darkened. Claiming to

> be wise, they became fools, and exchanged the glory of the
> immortal God for images resembling mortal man and birds
> and animals and creeping things (Rom. 1:18-23).

The above passage reveals that there's no such thing as an atheist. People who assert the claim that "there is no God" are simply suppressing the truth about the reality of His existence. Yet the external world of creation testifies to the existence of God as does the internal conviction of their own hearts! They know God exists, but they exchange this truth for a lie by exchanging the truth of God for their atheistic ideology (cf. Rom. 1:25). Therefore, both Paul and John can say that the denial of God is a lie, which leads to our final consideration.

The Perseverance of Absolute Truth

Thus far we've seen the reality of absolute truth and its suppression. Lastly, we want to consider the perseverance of absolute truth. One of the key words John uses throughout the second chapter of his letter is the term *abide*. This is a call for Christians to hold fast to the truth in order to remain faithful to the end. John reminds believers that the only way to persevere in this chaotic world is to cling to the truth that is in Jesus. He writes:

> Let what you heard from the beginning abide in you. If what
> you heard from the beginning abides in you, then you too will
> abide in the Son and in the Father. And this is the promise
> that he made to us—eternal life (1 John 2:24-25).

I don't have to tell you that the Christian life is hard. Living out our faith seems impossible at times, particularly in this cultural moment. Therefore, we need to hold even more firmly to the absolute and unchanging truths of God's Word for our survival if we're going to persevere faithfully to the end. We're called to "fight the good fight," and to finish the race to which we've been called amid life's many trials and temptations (1 Tim. 6:12). John next offers us three practical applications of this.

The first is found in 1 John 2:20: "But you have been anointed by the Holy One, and you all have knowledge." In the Bible, anointing is when a person is marked with oil and set apart for a unique task. Anointing represented that God was uniquely with that person and would equip them for the work He called them to do. The words "Christ" and "messiah" mean "anointed one." The anointing we receive is the gift of the Holy Spirit, the third person of the Trinity. He applies Christ's benefits to our lives, serves as our counselor by convicting us of sin and convincing us of truth, so when that moment of temptation does come, we're able to stand against the lie because the Spirit of God abides within us. That's why we need to pray daily, "Spirit of the living God, fall afresh on me."

In addition to the Holy Spirit's anointing, we have the Scriptures (1 John 2:24). We possess everything God intended us to know so that we would be "equipped for every good work" (2 Tim. 3:17). Therefore, we need churches that are committed to faithfully preaching God's Word in addition to offering many opportunities for Christians to grow in the grace and knowledge of our Lord. We must prioritize memorizing and meditating on God's Word—in order that we may faithfully persevere to the end. Parents and grandparents, we need to fortify our children and grandchildren for their battle against the allurements of this world.

And last, but not least, we need each other. In 1 John 2:19, the apostle informs us that many will come into the church, but they will not abide with us. John tells us the reason they won't abide with the church is because they were never true believers. Now, I'm not saying that some people who leave a church for whatever reason are automatically classified as *unbelievers*; sometimes sheep wander or get lost for a time. But what I am saying is that, ultimately, true believers will obey the command of Scripture not to neglect gathering with God's people. They will make worshipping God with the people of God a priority. I know this may be hard for some of us, especially for those who have little ones. It may seem like an almost impossible task to go to church weekly, but please don't buy into the lie of culture that diminishes the importance of our regular gatherings. Paul describes those who are removed from the church as a result of church discipline as those who have been "handed over to Satan" (1 Tim. 1:20). If we separate from the church and regular community with other believers, we will find ourselves in much greater danger of attack, confusion, and temptation. Please don't abandon God's family because this family is one of the primary means of grace you need in order to persevere. We need to encourage one another daily—and even more as we see the final day approaching (Heb. 10:24-25).

A Prayer for Truth to Be Revealed

Our Father and our God, I pray that your absolute, unchanging, objective truth would be the very thing that sets us free; that, Lord, we would not look to the empty philosophies and ways of this world in our search for freedom and hope, something the world can never provide. What we need is your absolute truth—that truth which alone gives us a firm foundation on which to build in a world that is constantly changing.

Perhaps there's someone reading this chapter who has never encountered this Jesus—maybe they've lived their lives suppressing the truth, trying to act as if you don't exist. Please open their eyes and soften their hearts so that they would no longer suppress the truth but rather receive the Truth, who became a man, Jesus Christ, who Himself said, "I am the Way, the Truth, and the Life. No one comes to the Father except through Me." May you rescue them, even at this very moment. May they discover real hope and experience true forgiveness from this time on and forevermore. We pray all these things in the name of Christ. Amen.

Application Questions

- Let's consider the nature of God and His relationship with truth. The world exists with time, in space, and is made of matter. This means that the God who created time, space, and matter must be beyond all those categories: eternal, without physical limitations, and immaterial.

  If God is like this, what does that mean for how we consider what is true or false? Can there be any "truth" that is independent of God in a world that God designed? If someone seeks to build their lives while rejecting God, what will their lives look like? What will their relationship to truth be?

- You'll often hear the idea that "times are changing" and our understanding of the world, morality, etc.

must change as well, if we are going to be "on the right side of history." When you hear this, what does it make you think? Why might this be a compelling idea for many people?

If God is the one who designed all things, this means that He is the only one who has the authority to define all things. If God is eternal and unchanging, how valid is the idea of ever-changing truth? Is it possible to be "on the right side of history" while rejecting God, who is the Lord and Judge of us all?

- Have you ever had a conversation with someone who you couldn't pin down? Even if you showed evidence to demonstrate what they thought was mistaken, they would just pivot or move the goalposts, and ignore what you said. There's an irony here: those who don't seem to care for the truth, or even deny its existence, are certain *they* have the truth.

  What seems to be the driving motivation for what such a person believes? If someone is confronted with the truth, but refuses to change their thinking, what does that reveal? How have you personally fought the truth when it was inconvenient or painful to acknowledge?

- Romans 1 says that all people know there is a God because He has made it plain to them through the creation itself, but instead of embracing that truth, they suppress it. In this sense, are there any real atheists? How should this impact the way we do evangelism?

As people suppress the truth they know about God, Romans says that God gives them over to a depraved mind; that is, He lets them embrace further falsehood and confusion as they continually reject Him. In this sense, are we dealing with mere "differences of opinion," or is rejecting the truth a sin? Are there truths in God's Word that you are aware of, which you have been suppressing? What falsehoods have you embraced for self-centered reasons, which God is calling you to repent of?

- Jesus says, "If you abide in my word, you are truly my disciples, and you will know the truth, and the truth will set you free" (John 8:31-32). This is a recurring theme in the Bible, from the very beginning. When Adam and Eve fell, they did not honestly approach God, but sought to hide themselves under fig leaves in their fear. But God is not impressed with or tricked by any of our coverings. He is waiting in the heart of the garden and we only begin to experience real relationship with Him when we come to Him, recognizing that we are naked and ashamed.

How would your life change if, instead of raging at difficult truths or trying to obscure the truth so you don't have to face it, you committed to being fully honest with God, with yourself, and with those in your life?

5

The Problem of Sin

Every human being knows the weight of regret. We've all felt that sick feeling in the pit of our stomachs after saying words we can't take back, or the crushing shame of actions that haunt us years later. But beyond these personal wounds lies an even deeper tragedy—sin has fractured the very foundation of our world, vandalizing God's good creation and severing the intimate relationship we were meant to have with our Creator. Like a stone thrown into still waters, the ripples of sin spread outward endlessly, touching every aspect of human existence with its corruption and leaving us longing for restoration. The exploration of this reality is important because without a clear understanding of what the Bible teaches about sin and the fall of humanity, many things that occur in your personal life and the world will make little sense.

In fact, not knowing the truth about sin can cause a lot of damage, both to us and to those around us. The Bible's teaching on sin challenges our culture's notions on self-esteem by offering an accurate assessment of the true nature of our humanity. Let's look at what the apostle Paul has to say in Romans 3:9-20:

> What then? Are we Jews any better off? No, not at all. For we have already charged that all, both Jews and Greeks, are under sin, as it is written: "None is righteous, no, not one; no one understands; no one seeks for God. All have turned aside; together they have become worthless; no one does good, not even one." "Their throat is an open grave; they use their tongues to deceive." "The venom of asps is under their lips." "Their mouth is full of curses and bitterness." "Their feet are swift to shed blood; in their paths are ruin and misery, and the way of peace they have not known." "There is no fear of God before their eyes." Now we know that whatever the law says it speaks to those who are under the law, so that every mouth may be stopped, and the whole world may be held accountable to God. For by works of the law no human being will be justified in his sight, since through the law comes knowledge of sin.

Indeed, each of us—no person or society excepted—is born under the yolk of sin and lives amid the consequences of it. Thus, we are well served to reflect on sin as a multi-faceted horror.

The Universal Problem of Sin

The first thing to observe is that sin is a very serious problem of universal proportions. All humanity stands guilty before God—both Jew and Greek alike. What Paul states here would have been particularly offensive to a Jewish person living in the first century because many were very religious and believed they were acceptable to God based on their good works. The Greeks, on the other hand, may have been religious; but from a Jewish perspective, they were unacceptable because they worshipped false deities. So, here

Paul levels the playing field by exposing the reality of the situation: Everyone stands guilty under the scrutinous eyes of the one to whom we must give an account (Rom. 3:19). This is the universal problem of sin.

You see, Romans 3:9-20 teaches that sin is a very serious problem because of its universal proportions. It's not as if we can point the finger and say, "It's those people out there," because you and I are "those people." We all stand guilty before a holy God to whom we must give an account.

The Systemic Effects of Sin

We often hear the word "systemic" in discussions across multiple media platforms. It's a term coined by the global elite in their attempt to change Western culture by claiming they have the answer to the root problem of our society. We've heard talk about the "systemic" problem of our history, the "systemic" problems of our forefathers, nation, and culture. And we would agree that there is a systemic problem—but not just with Western culture. It's a global problem, one that truly relates to the entire system of mankind.

The so-called systemic problems of Western culture didn't begin in 1619; they began much earlier. These problems began in a garden when our first parents rebelled against their holy Creator. Sin corrupted Adam and Eve, and that original sin had a corrupting influence over every culture produced by human beings from that day forward because human beings are the primary shapers of culture. Thus, until we understand the systemic nature of sin as the mother root of all our problems, we'll never begin to understand the brokenness we experience in this fallen world. The systemic problems created by sinful human beings are, indeed, a global problem.

None Righteous

Not only do we see the universal, systemic nature of sin, but we see also its destructive effects. Romans 3:10 declares that "No one is righteous, no, not one." What Paul says here is that we've been separated from God because of our sin, and none of us have the power within ourselves to produce a perfect moral righteousness that would enable us to stand before a holy and just God. None of us can be "justified" (declared righteous and acceptable) according to God's standards because none of us have kept His law perfectly; "No one is righteous, no, not one." This is what theologians have called "total depravity." The fall of humanity has affected us to the very core of our being.

Paul begins with the statement that "no one understands; no one seeks for God" (Rom. 3:11). In verses 11-18, he continues by stringing together a series of Old Testament texts, graphically describing the destructive effects of sin, thus demonstrating the nature and degree of human depravity. And this is tragic because we were created to be in relationship with Him—to glorify God and enjoy Him forever. But instead, we've become alienated from God because of our sin and have no interest in being reconciled. Rather, we're seeking to be a master of our own life, and what a miserable life that is: "All have turned aside; together they have become worthless; no one does good, not even one" (Rom. 3:12).

Some may be thinking that they know a lot of people who say and do good things, but they aren't Christian, and this may be true. I know people like that as well. But the questions are, "What are they really like *on the inside*? What are the real motivations of their hearts? Are their words and deeds motivated to bring God glory, or are they motivated to bring glory to themselves?" According to Scripture (and our own experience) you and I would have to admit that the latter is the case. So, even the good things that non-Christians do are hopelessly self-centered.[1]

Practical Implications

Now some may be saying to themselves, "I know this, but where is the gospel?" Don't worry, it's coming. Sin will not have the last word. But in seeking to cultivate a truly biblical worldview it's imperative that we understand the Bible's teaching on this important subject, without which we'll never be able to make sense of the tragic events that have happened in the world and are presently occurring in our own time.

For example, when we tune in to the news, we find ourselves bombarded with negativity. Often we hear terrible things and wonder how humanity could be so cruel. Why would people commit such atrocities? How can they be so evil? The affairs of this world and the current events of our time don't make sense without an understanding of the Bible's teaching about sin.

The same is true for our personal lives. None of us are exempt from suffering and tragedy. But the question is, when these things intrude into your life, do you have the biblical framework in which to interpret them? Without the biblical doctrine of sin, tragedy and suffering will never make sense. You'll always be asking yourself, "Why is this happening to me? Why do I have to go through this? Why

---

1 There's so much more to unpack regarding sin's destructive effects, but the constraints of this chapter don't permit me to do so. I recommend the excellent book by Philip Ryken, *Christian Worldview: A Student's Guide* (Wheaton: Crossway, 2013), and particularly the chapter "Paradise Lost." In my view, it's one of the best summaries on the subject.

do I feel like my life is under a dark cloud right now?" If we don't understand the reality of sin and its destructive effects, there's no way we'll survive. An understanding of the biblical doctrine of sin offers us the only way to survive personal tragedy and suffering.

Understanding the biblical doctrine of sin also enables us to make sense of the gospel. Why in the world would God send His only begotten Son to die for us, unless there was no other way? Unless He looked upon humanity and saw us as we truly are—utterly helpless in our state of sin? Fully grasping how good the *good* news is can only come from first understanding how bad the *bad* news is. If we don't have a robust biblical understanding of sin, then the grace of God that comes to us through the gospel will never be amazing. And this leads to our final point.

The Only Remedy for Sin

There is only one remedy for sin. For you see, Romans 3 doesn't just describe people who are sick; it describes people who are under the judgment of death! Now we know that the only person who can change the situation is God, if indeed He's willing—and He *is* willing! God so loved the world that He gave His only begotten Son to be the sacrifice for our sins and to provide the moral righteousness that we can't provide for ourselves:

> But now the righteousness of God has been manifested apart from the law, although the Law and the Prophets bear witness to it—the righteousness of God through faith in Jesus Christ for all who believe. For there is no distinction: for all have sinned and fall short of the glory of God and are justified by his grace as a gift through the redemption that is in Christ Jesus, whom God put forward as a *propitiation* by his blood,

to be received by faith. This was to show God's righteousness, because in his divine forbearance he had passed over former sins. It was to show his righteousness at the present time, so that he might be just and the justifier of the one who has faith in Jesus. (Rom. 3:21-26, emphasis mine)

A key word in Romans 3:25 is *propitiation*. This term is connected to the Old Testament sacrificial system, and particularly with reference to the annual Day of Atonement. This was a very special day in the life of the Israelites in which the high priest would enter the most holy place of the tabernacle with the blood of a spotless sacrifice to make atonement (satisfaction and removal) for the sins of God's people (Lev. 16). With the blood sprinkled on the ark of the covenant, the sins committed by the people that year were forgiven.

By using this term, Paul is telling us that the sacrifice of Jesus has not only fulfilled this sacrifice, but that all the Old Testament sacrifices pointed to and were fulfilled in Him! Moreover, this tremendous gift of God's grace is not just for the Jewish people. It's available to everyone who puts their faith in Jesus Christ!

Since the problem and effects of sin are universal, so is God's merciful and extravagant remedy: God so loved the world that He gave his only begotten Son to be the propitiatory sacrifice for our sins so that all who believe in Him can receive forgiveness and be declared righteous as the gracious gift of God.

This, my friends, is the good news of the gospel. "He made him to be sin who knew no sin, so that in him we might become the righteousness of God" (2 Cor. 5:21). And again, "For everyone who calls on the name of the Lord will be saved" (Rom. 10:13). Have you put your faith in Jesus?

An Amazing Rescue

In 2010, an earthquake ravaged the city of Port-au-Prince and its surrounding areas. A pastor's house fell during the quake and a little girl was trapped under the debris. For days her rescuers could hear her crying but couldn't find her. On the fifth day, they no longer heard her crying, so they began to clean up the remaining debris. Then suddenly, they heard her voice again, crying out, "Daddy! Be careful. I'm still under here." And she was rescued.

You and I were in a very similar situation. We were trapped under the house of sin by nature. And just like that little girl who couldn't rescue herself—you and I by nature can't rescue ourselves. The biblical teaching on sin reminds us that we can't rescue ourselves, but we do have one who can. We have one who has already done the heavy lifting for us. So don't abandon the hope of the gospel. There's no other explanation or remedy for the brokenness of our lives and the world. May we, as the people of God, in every generation, continue to hold out this hope in answering the call to be salt and light amid the darkness. And if you haven't already called upon the Lord for salvation, don't hold off any longer. Respond to His rescuing call now.

A Prayer of Confession and Hope

Holy and merciful Father, we come before you as sinners, acutely aware of how our rebellion has vandalized your good creation and wounded our own souls. We confess that we have chosen our way over yours countless times, allowing pride, selfishness, and desire to rule our hearts rather than your perfect will. The very sins we hate, we continue to commit; the good we long to do often remains undone. Yet we thank you that this is not the end of our story.

In your great mercy, you sent your Son to bear our sins and break their power. We praise you that where sin increased, your grace abounded all the more. Lord Jesus, we cling to your cross, where our guilt was paid in full and our shame was washed away. Holy Spirit, continue your sanctifying work in us, transforming our hearts and renewing our minds until we reflect more fully the image of Christ. Though sin's presence grieves us now, we rejoice in the promise that one day you will make all things new, and we will know the glorious freedom of being fully conformed to your likeness. Until that day, keep us walking in repentance and faith, confident in your forgiveness and empowered by your grace. In Jesus' name, Amen.

Application Questions

- If the effects of sin are so great, as Paul describes in Romans 3, what danger is there in assuming that we aren't really that bad or that we are naturally righteous? If we have a very high view of our own ability and goodness, how will that affect our approach to repentance?

- Very often, people will say, "I'm a good person" and then compare themselves to someone truly horrific (Hitler, Stalin, etc.). While it's true that most people will never be guilty of the same sorts of evil as men who slaughtered millions, are we going to be judged by God based on how we compare to the worst people we can think of? Just because we are less

HOW FIRM A FOUNDATION

sinful than Hitler, is that the same thing as being innocent or righteous?

God regularly commands that perfection is His standard (Lev. 11:44-45, 19:2; Matt. 5:48, etc.). If perfection is the standard, where does that leave all of humanity?

- The Pharisees' greatest sin was pride in their own moral rectitude when, in fact, they were wholly blind to how desperately disobedient they were. It was their self-righteous sense of self that caused them to separate from *those* sorts of people.

  Consider the doctrine of total depravity. If your mind is occupied by how terrible the sin of others is, how might the doctrine help you to overcome your own self-righteousness? If God calls us to minister to the lost and call them to new life, how does a self-righteous attitude destroy one's ability to fulfill that mission?

- Perhaps you—or someone you know—struggles with an overwhelming sense of guilt and shame. Some who carry this shame feel they cannot let go of their past, and it continually affects their daily life. How might this constant self-deprecation be a sign that they believe there really are individuals who are good enough to save themselves—and that simply is not them? How might the doctrine of total depravity be a blessing that helps to free individuals from this unchecked guilt?

- The bad news of the doctrine of sin is that none of us can save ourselves. The good news, however, is that God has done everything necessary in order that people, just like us, can be saved! God doesn't simply leave us where we started.

Read Romans 12:1-2 and Ephesians 2:8-10. What does Paul say the result of our salvation will be? Although we were naturally fallen, how does God change us? Repentance means to turn around. How do these passages give us true hope that we can and will grow in obedience, leaving our sinful habits behind?

- Prior to our salvation, the law of God works to condemn us. Paul says that it is through the law that we become aware that we are guilty, which causes us to cry out to God for redemption (Romans 7:7-8). After we are saved, however, the law of God becomes a guide, enabling us to understand what God regards as good and righteous.

Read Romans 8:1-17. What does Paul say about those who commit themselves to obeying their flesh? On the contrary, what is the result of those who walk according to the Spirit? As someone who is filled with the Spirit, how should this motivate and provide hope for you in your fight against sin?

6

Jesus, the Only Way to God

In a world celebrating diversity and championing multiple paths to truth, the claim that Jesus Christ is the only way to God can sound jarring, even offensive. Sophisticated people in the twenty-first century often view such exclusive claims with skepticism, dismissing them as relics of a less enlightened age. Yet what if the most rational position, the one most consistent with evidence and human experience, is that Jesus of Nazareth truly was God in human flesh? What if the historical reality of His life, death, and resurrection presents us not with blind faith, but with a reasonable foundation for believing that He alone can bridge the gap between humanity and God? The extraordinary claim that God became human to rescue us is either history's greatest hoax or its most profound truth—and the evidence compels us to consider the latter with utmost seriousness.

This chapter builds upon these truths by showing that Jesus is not one of many ways to God, but as He Himself has said, He *is the only way*. Let's look at John 14:1-6:

Let not your hearts be troubled. Believe in God; believe also in me. In my Father's house are many rooms. If it were not so, would I have told you that I go to prepare a place for you? And if I go and prepare a place for you, I will come again and will take you to myself, that where I am you may be also. And you know the way to where I am going." Thomas [doubting Thomas] said to him, "Lord, we do not know where you are going. How can we know the way?" Jesus said to him, "I am the way, and the truth, and the life. No one comes to the Father except through me.

This passage takes place on the eve of Jesus' betrayal and arrest. Jesus is in the process of preparing His disciples for His impending return to the Father after He completes His work on the cross. Although Jesus doesn't specifically mention the cross, He certainly alludes to it. Much of what He says is difficult for His disciples to comprehend. They don't understand why He must leave, why it is that they can't go with Him. It's within this context that Jesus tells them that He is the Way, the Truth, and the Life, and that no one comes to the Father apart from Him.

Even though the disciples didn't understand the full import of what Jesus was saying, I suspect that His words brought some comfort to those whose lives had just been turned upside down—comfort in the fact that they had already believed in the one who is the Way, the Truth, and the Life.

But what about us?

Some may be wondering how this chapter applies to them. Like the disciples, you already believe in Jesus, and you're convinced that Christianity is the only true faith. So how might this chapter inform your life?

One of the first things to draw your attention to is the fact that the church is under rigorous assault. Secular humanism is on the rise.[1] We're bombarded daily by various educational, political, and media platforms seeking to silence us in the marketplace of ideas as they work to eradicate the true Christian faith from the world. You might hear things like, "Keep your Christianity to yourself. It has no place in public society," and so forth.

Thus, if you are a true believer, I write with the hopeful prayer that I might encourage and assure you concerning your faith, particularly regarding Jesus' own teaching that He is the Way, the Truth, and the Life. I hope to encourage and assure you that God is the supreme reality and there is no other way to be reconciled to Him except by faith in the person and work of His beloved Son.

Now for others who may be skeptical about Christianity or are perhaps doubting its claims to truth: Perhaps you're reading this and find yourself doubting, just like Thomas, who was one of Jesus' original disciples. If you're in either one of those categories (skeptical or doubting), let me say that I'm glad you're reading this. Here is a challenge for you: Suspend your skepticism and doubt for a moment in order to ask yourself, "Do I really understand what I'm rejecting? Do I really understand what I'm doubting about Christianity?"

Here's the bottom line: There's no such thing as an unbeliever. Everyone believes in something. My prayer for you as you read is that you would be firmly convinced that Jesus is truly the only way to God and that the message offered in Christianity is the only reasonable and rational expression of true faith.

---

1 thegospelcoalition.org/article/9-things-secular-humanism/

The Claim of Christianity

So what is the claim of Christianity? What is one of its cardinal tenets that makes it so controversial and deemed by many as countercultural, even in Jesus' own time? The obvious answer is its exclusivity. Greco-Roman culture, like our own, was tolerant of many belief systems, but it wasn't tolerant about exclusive claims to faith. Jesus claims to be the exclusive way to God. And the reason He can say this is because He isn't only a rabbi or a teacher of the truth; He is Truth incarnate! What Jesus is saying, therefore, is that the way is not found in polytheism, nor does it lie in a karmic path, religious ceremonialism, or secular humanism. The way to the Father is solely through the person and work of His Son, Jesus.

The Objections

Now some will reject the claims that Jesus is the only way to God and that Christianity is the only true religion, but they typically do so based on *ad hominem* arguments.[2] For example, they may call Christians arrogant for making such an exclusive claim. We are often called "primitive and unsophisticated"—and even "a danger to society."[3]

Yet sadly, some Christians are being influenced by this line of faulty and deceptive reasoning. It may cause them to question the truth they've been taught. They may say things to themselves like, "Maybe there's something to this. Maybe we need to broaden our message. Maybe we need to soften

---

2 that is, attacking an opponents character rather than their argument.

3 These ad hominem arguments were active in the first century, even as they are in our own time. See michaeljkruger.com/let-them-not-share-in-the-affairs-of-life-how-ancient-christians-were-viewed-as-dangerous-to-society/.

the gospel. Maybe we need a message that's just a little more inclusive and not so difficult and narrow."

Another way that Christianity's exclusiveness comes under attack is by the assertion that all religions are equal because they basically teach the same thing. Perhaps you've heard the mountain illustration in which there are various paths to take in order to reach the top; in this illustration, all paths lead to the same destination. But a serious look into the belief systems of the major world religions reveals that each of these religions couldn't be more different. There may be some overlapping themes, but the basic tenets of these faiths are different and should be recognized as such. Moreover, not only are they different, but the ironic thing is, all the major world religions make the same claim to exclusivity![4] So, if a fair dialogue were really taking place, we would be asking, "Why aren't followers of these other religions derided as arrogant, primitive and unsophisticated for being exclusive? Why is Christianity singled out?"

Or perhaps you've heard someone say that all religions have part of the truth, but not the whole truth. This argument assumes that now, over the course of thousands of years, we've "evolved" to such a state as to have arrived at *the truth*. Here's another irony: the "truth" that postmodernism has arrived at is that there is *no absolute truth*. Therefore, there is no exclusive way, as far as we know. But you and I know that this view is simply not true![5]

On the surface of things, these objections may sound humble, but they're not. They're deceptive. You see, the reality

---

4   christianapologeticsalliance.com/2017/08/02/exclusivity-claims-major-world-religions/

5   thegospelcoalition.org/themelios/article/the-biblical-view-of-truth-challenges-postmodernist-truth-decay/

is that everyone—regardless of what they believe—has an exclusive faith. Everyone claims some level of exclusivity; even the person who says there's no such thing as absolute truth is making an absolute claim to truth. Everyone who claims all religions lead to the same destination actually believes that they know everything there is to know in the world, enough to deny that any religion specifically teaches the truth. They claim that every religion reaches the same destination by different paths up the mountain because *they believe they can see the whole mountain, while no one else does.* Ironically, if you ask them how much time they have spent studying Christianity, Judaism, Islam, Hinduism, or Buddhism, etc., you'll often discover that they are universally ignorant, having spent no time studying *any* religion with seriousness. Nevertheless, despite knowing less about any religion than a young child raised in these faiths, they purportedly know enough to confidently declare that there is no absolute truth. That, my friends, is the epitome of arrogance masquerading as if it were humility—the very thing Christians are often accused of.

The real question is not who believes in truth and who doesn't believe in truth. Everyone, at some level, believes in some brand of truth that is exclusive. The real question is, what is *the real truth*? And we've already provided the answer to that question: Truth is a person. He is the Lord Jesus Christ. These truth claims make Christianity more than a religion. In fact, it's unlike any religion or belief system in the world.

Jesus Is Unique
If it's true that Christianity is the only true way, what's the evidence for it? The evidence is Jesus Himself.

Claiming a divine identity was rather common in the ancient world, particularly for rulers seeking absolute authority. The Pharaohs of Egypt and Roman emperors were all hailed as god-kings, but it's one thing for a man to claim he is God and another to prove it. It's common for critics of Christianity to say that Jesus never said He was God and that His divinity was a later add-on by His followers. This, however, is categorically false. The divine identity of Christ is revealed as we consider three distinct truths.

Son of God

The title "son of God" is not unique in the Bible and isn't, in itself, a claim of divinity. Adam and his descendants, God's people as a whole, and Solomon are called sons of God (Luke 3:38; Gen. 6:2; Exod. 4:22; 2 Sam. 7:14). However, Jesus is presented as the Son of God in a unique sense. When the angel came to Mary, he said,

> "Do not be afraid, Mary, for you have found favor with God. And behold, you will conceive in your womb and bear a son, and you shall call his name Jesus. He will be great and will be called the Son of the Most High. And the Lord God will give to him the throne of his father David."
>
> And Mary said to the angel, "How will this be, since I am a virgin?"
>
> And the angel answered her, "The Holy Spirit will come upon you, and the power of the Most High will overshadow you; therefore the child to be born will be called holy—the Son of God" (Luke 1:30-32, 34-35).

Jesus is the son of David and, therefore, destined for kingship. But, even more, He is God's Son—born in human nature only because God intervened to cause Mary, a virgin, to conceive without human involvement. Jesus, unlike any other man who might be called the son of God, was not merely a chosen king whom God *treated* like a son, but Jesus is the only man born from a virgin. Only Jesus is the *eternal* Son.

Equality and Unity with the Father

If you are someone's child, that means you are like them. You share their features, their name, their identity, their characteristics. Jesus regularly claimed, as the Son of God, that He was the unique representative of the Father and like Him in a way no one else was. The religious leaders of Israel sought to kill Jesus because He claimed God as Father, which meant that he was "making himself equal with God" (John 5:18). And Jesus did, indeed, claim just that:

> Truly, truly, I say to you, the Son can do nothing of his own accord, but only what he sees the Father doing. For whatever the Father does, that the Son does likewise. For the Father loves the Son and shows him all that he himself is doing. And greater works than these will he show him, so that you may marvel. For as the Father raises the dead and gives them life, so also the Son gives life to whom he will. For the Father judges no one, but has given all judgment to the Son, that all may honor the Son, just as they honor the Father. Whoever does not honor the Son does not honor the Father who sent him. Truly, truly, I say to you, whoever hears my word and believes him who sent me has eternal life (John 5:19-24).

Jesus claimed identical authority to God the Father because He and the Father shared the same divinity—the same nature and being—and because Jesus is divine He declares, "I and the Father are one" (John 10:30). As they "picked up stones to stone him, [they said], 'It is not for a good work that we are going to stone you but for blasphemy, because you, being a man, make yourself God'" (John 10:31, 33). And Jesus replied, "If I am not doing the works of my Father, then do not believe me; but if I do them, even though you do not believe me, believe the works, that you may know and understand that the Father is in me and I am in the Father" (John 10:37-38).

To know Jesus is to know God because they are one and the same.

The Great I AM

Even those with little familiarity with the Bible remember that when Moses asked for God's name, God referred to Himself with the name "I AM" (Exod. 3:13-14). Out of a desire to honor God's name by not using it needlessly, the Jews most often referred to God as *Adonai*, which means Lord. Jesus is often referred to as "the Lord" (Luke 2:11; John 11:27, etc.), but Jesus also referred to Himself many times with the phrase "I AM."

When the crowds clamored in their starvation for bread that Jesus could provide, He said, "I am the bread of life" (John 6:35). Referencing the manna from heaven with which God fed the Israelites in the wilderness, Jesus said, "[T]he bread of God is he who comes down from heaven and gives life to the world … I am the bread of life; whoever comes to me shall not hunger, and whoever believes in me shall never thirst" (John 6:33, 35). Jesus is the "I AM." His existence is eternal.

To the Pharisees, Jesus proclaimed, "I am the light of the world… You are from below; I am from above. You are of this world; I am not of this world" (John 8:12, 23). Here Jesus makes reference to the very beginning of creation, when

God said, "Let there be light." Light is part of the creation, but Jesus claims that He is the true light—the source of all light, God Himself.

Jesus spoke another "I am" as he criticized the Pharisees and priests for their faithlessness: "Truly, truly, I say to you, I am the door of the sheep ... I am the good shepherd. The good shepherd lays down his life for the sheep" (John 10:7, 11). Jesus identifies Himself as the means by which anyone enters into God's fold and, referencing Psalm 23, identifies Himself with the God of Israel: "The Lord is my shepherd, I shall not want" (Psalm 23:1).

Yet another "I am" statement of Jesus uses a grape vine metaphor: "I am the true vine ... the branch cannot bear fruit, unless it abides in the vine, [and] neither can you" (John 15:1, 4). Jesus declares that He is the very source of all spiritual vitality, from which all good fruit that we might bear comes.

Perhaps the clearest example is when Jesus was disputing with a group of Jews who claimed that they were truly Abraham's sons, despite not believing in Jesus. "Jesus said to them, 'If you were Abraham's children, you would be doing the works that Abraham did, but now you seek to kill me... Your father Abraham rejoiced that he would see my day'" (John 8:39-40, 56). They responded, "You are not yet fifty years old, and have seen Abraham?" To which Jesus answered, "'Truly, truly, I say to you, before Abraham was, *I am*.' So they picked up stones to throw at him" (John 8:57-59). They understood what He meant and, as always, sought to kill Him for it. Jesus was saying that He is the great I AM, with an existence far beyond His mortal life as the thirty-three-year-old son of Mary.

Finally, if all the above claims are true, this final claim makes much more sense: "I am the way, the truth, and the life. No come comes to the Father except through me" (John 14:6). Jesus is the only means to God because He is God the Son, the second person of the Trinity, and He was born as the perfect revelation of God in human form. In Christ, God became like humanity in order to give His life so that our sins would be forgiven. To say that Christianity is the only way to God is to simply acknowledge what God has done in Jesus.

But, again, it's one thing to claim to be God and another thing altogether to prove it. And here we come to the crux of the issue: everything hinges on the resurrection. The apostle Paul said the resurrection is the heart of everything:

> [I]f there is no resurrection of the dead, then not even Christ has been raised. And if Christ has not been raised, then *our preaching is in vain and your faith is in vain.* We are even found [guilty of] misrepresenting God, because we testified about God that he raised Christ [from the dead] … [I]f Christ has not been raised, your faith is futile and you are still in your sins … [and] *we are of all people most to be pitied.* (1 Cor. 15:13-15, 17, 19)

It's one thing to claim to be God. It's one thing to work miracles and heal the sick—there are witch doctors and gurus who possess powers not easily explained or understood, who seem to be able to do just that—but no one comes back from the dead of their own accord. If Jesus claimed to be God, claimed to be the Savior of the world, and predicted that He would be "delivered into the hands of sinful men and be crucified and on the third day rise," and then He *did it*—that demonstrates that His claims are true (Luke 24:7). If Jesus claimed all these things and *then* defeated death itself, that means that God has vindicated Jesus' claims just as Jesus said He would.

Still, there are many who will say that the disciples merely stole His body and made the whole story up for personal gain. But the Gospels tell us what the disciples did when Jesus was crucified—they ran for their lives, some even denying they ever knew Him, because they knew they could end up crucified on a cross the next day. But *something happened* which caused them all to change. *Something happened* that caused these fearful men to become utterly courageous, willing to stand before the very men who put Jesus on that cross and to say, "Jesus Christ of Nazareth, whom you crucified ... God raised from the dead [and] there is salvation in no one else" (Acts 4:10, 12).

They made it up for personal gain? What *gain*? The message they preached was one of self-sacrifice, abandoning worldly wealth for the pursuit of righteousness, abandoning fleshly pursuits for the sake of holiness. If selfish men were crafting a religion, they would have taught it was permissible to conquer by the sword and take married women as your wives, or that heaven was a place of never-ending sex with virgins, like the false prophet Muhammad did. But the disciples, instead, refused to raise swords to plunder and were instead routinely beaten, arrested, stoned, and reviled wherever they went. Every one of Christ's disciples were willing to suffering and die, if it came to it, for teaching that Jesus had been raised from the dead and, therefore, proved that He is the Lord of all. Those who claim they made it all up for the sake of worldly gain have clearly never considered anything they actually said.

But even more, it would be one thing for Jesus' followers to have a change of heart, but His *enemies* came to acknowledge His resurrection as well. Paul, who went on to write most of the books in the New Testament, was an early persecutor of the church. When Stephen, the first martyr of the church, was stoned to death, Paul (Saul) stood by watching with approval. Jesus had told His disciples that when they prayed in His name, He would answer them from heaven (John 14:12-14). Stephen prayed with his dying breath, "Lord Jesus, receive my spirit [and] do not hold this sin against them" (Acts 7:59-60).

While on his way to Damascus to arrest the Christians there for preaching that Jesus was the Savior, Paul was struck blind when Jesus appeared to him, saying, "Why are you persecuting me … I am Jesus, whom you are persecuting" (Acts 9:4-5). But when a disciple of Jesus prayed for Paul to receive back his sight, he was healed. And from that day, Paul spent his life preaching that Jesus is God and Lord, and the only Savior of all men.

Importantly, Paul doesn't merely ask us to trust his word. He encouraged people to check the facts, saying, Jesus "appeared to more than five hundred brothers at one time, most of whom are still alive" (1 Cor. 15:6). Those who claim that the resurrected appearances of Jesus were hallucinations aren't paying attention. Hallucinations aren't shared, they're *individual* events. But because Paul saw Jesus face to face— because more than five hundred had seen Jesus face to face—he was willing to abandon everything he believed and all the prestige he had gained as a persecutor of the church. Paul was persuaded to stake his life on Jesus, the one whom he had hated, whose followers he had helped to kill. Paul was beheaded in Rome for preaching this very message. But as he said, his sufferings were worth it because "this light momentary affliction is preparing for us an eternal weight of glory beyond all comparison" (2 Cor. 4:17). Because of Jesus, Paul said, we have become "heirs of God and fellow heirs with Christ, provided we suffer [as Jesus suffered] in order that we may also be glorified with him" (Rom. 8:17).

Ask yourself—would you be willing to be tortured to death for something you *knew* you made up? As it has been said, liars don't make good martyrs. Terrorists may fly into buildings, killing themselves and others, because they were deceived into believing a lie. That's something altogether different from being willing to be killed because you know what you saw with your own eyes—personally, face to face.

Jesus claimed to be God. He claimed to be the world's Savior. He predicted His death and resurrection. And then He came back to life on the third day and the world has been transformed as a result.

Amazing Grace

Isn't it amazing that at this moment in John's Gospel, in John 14, the moment of the disciples' deep distress, Jesus didn't say something like, "Believe whatever you want to believe as long as it brings you comfort, as long as it makes you happy"? No. Jesus told His disciples what they needed to hear—the truth. And the beautiful thing is that after He had accomplished His cross work, they would be commissioned to take that message into a dark world that so desperately needs to hear that same truth.

As I write this, I'm thinking about Christian students who are about to enter college or university. Let me warn you that you're about to be confronted by professors who will challenge your commitment to Jesus Christ. Some will seek to undo your faith while others will try to convince you of the need to soften or broaden the Christian message. Please don't fall for it. To affirm the true Christian faith is the most consistent and humble position to be in. Jesus *is* God and, therefore, He alone has the right to define the way to God.

This is what makes Christianity unique. Other religions say, "I have the truth and I can be saved by performing that truth." Christianity declares that truth has come down in the person of Jesus Christ, and He has come to set us free from slavery to sin. We'll never be able to live well enough to achieve salvation. That's the whole point. Jesus became our substitute. Out of His love for God and for us, He lived a perfectly righteous life before the Father. He died the death of deaths so that we don't have to, and He rose again that we might have abundant life, both now and forevermore. This is the message of Christianity.

Do not be ashamed of the gospel. Never be afraid to say, "I am a Christian, and I am saved by God's grace alone—and God has given no other name but Jesus by which we can be saved." Don't back down, because this world is in desperate need for your light to shine amid a dark and decaying world.

And do you know the amazing thing? Some may be thinking, "If I don't soften the message of the gospel no one will believe it." Don't forget our previous chapter: God is sovereign and salvation is a work of the Holy Spirit. God is the one who opens our hearts when the gospel is preached—so preach it! And look what happened to the church in the first century. It exploded! The world was turned upside down: Women worshipping with men, Jews worshipping with Gentiles, slaves coming to see that they were beloved to God even as the world treats them with contempt, prostitutes and tax collectors streaming into the Kingdom of God. The exclusive message of Christianity produced the world's most radical, inclusive community ever—wherein everyone, regardless of race, gender, or social status was welcomed and continues to be welcomed. In fact, the early church was originally called "the Way."[6] Why? Because Jesus Christ is the only way to the Father, the only way to be reconciled to God, and Jesus' way is the only way to true peace among men.

For all the prodigals floating through life with no sense of purpose or direction, I have a message for you, too: It's never too late to come home. Won't you do so right now? Right now, wherever you are, you can talk to God and simply say, "I am ready to come home. I am a sinner who's ready to receive your grace."

I tell you today, Jesus is alive and you have every opportunity to know Him, just as you might know anyone else. If you know that you aren't perfect in your obedience to God, if you know that you need help in this life, and you *think* Jesus might even have been raised from the dead, cry out to Him. Everyone who calls upon the name of Jesus will never be put to shame.

A Prayer to Come Home

Our God and Father, for all who have tried every form of self-improvement method, may they stop and surrender today and embrace the exclusive message of Christianity that declares that through faith in Jesus Christ they can be saved by simply praying a prayer like this:

---

6 See Acts 9:2, 19:23, 22:4, 24:14.

Jesus, I surrender. Jesus, I lay my life down. I'm tired and weary. But now I know today for the first time that I no longer must climb up. You have come down. You left your throne above, taking on the form of a servant and laying down your life for sinners such as me. I believe in you—I believe that you died for my sins and rose for my justification. And I receive you as my Savior and Lord not because of anything I have done, but by the free gift of salvation that is found in you alone. Take my burden; take my shame; take my sin. I receive your salvation. Cleanse me and clothe me in your righteousness, both now and forevermore. Amen.

Application Questions

- We have the benefit of knowing the end of Jesus' story, but the disciples did not. Read the passage at the beginning of the chapter. What was Jesus trying to do for His disciples? What comfort and strength might they have received had they remembered His words?

- How have you seen individuals in your own life seek to deny that any religion has an exclusive corner on the truth? What do you think would motivate someone from holding to this belief? What is it about the exclusivity of Christianity that makes people squirm so much?

- Consider the image of religions as different paths up the same mountain. How does this idea deny the claims of all religions? When someone claims to know that no religion has the full truth, what kind of knowledge are *they* claiming to have? Is this truly a position of humility, or something else?

- Consider the various ways that Jesus claimed to be God. What stands out to you about the way Jesus spoke of Himself? Are there any particular instances that you find most compelling—why? With someone making these kinds of claims, what are your options for response?

- Paul said that if Jesus wasn't raised from the dead, our preaching and faith are worthless. Why does the resurrection mean so much for Christianity? How does the resurrection of Jesus prove, beyond a shadow of a doubt, that what Jesus claimed was true? If Jesus was raised from the dead, what does that mean about your sins?

- And what about you? What difficulties are you facing in your life? How does the truthfulness of Christianity provide you with hope and a firm foundation? If Jesus was raised from the dead, though He was killed by the government and rejected by His own people, what does that mean for your own trials? Is Jesus worthy of your trust as you "walk through the valley of the shadow of death" (Ps. 23:4)?

7

The Deity of Jesus Christ

Many people would probably agree that Jesus was the most influential figure ever to live. But why? What was it about Him? His teaching? It was more than His teaching because He was more than a man. Jesus was and forever will be the God-man. His life, death, resurrection, and ascension have completely changed human history forever, and we continue to experience the transformative effects of His work even up to our day. In what follows, we'll be considering two primary things about Jesus and how these underscore His deity: Who He is and what He did. In so doing, we'll be looking at select verses from John 1:1-18:[1]

> In the beginning was the Word, and the Word was with God, and the Word was God. He was in the beginning with God. All things were made through him, and without him was not anything made that was made. In him was life, and the life

---

[1] You're already familiar with this passage of Scripture from our chapter on origins where we discussed why the biblical teaching about creation matters. The focus of this chapter will uncover what John's prologue has to say concerning the deity of Jesus Christ.

was the light of men. The light shines in the darkness, and the darkness has not overcome it ... The true light, which gives light to everyone, was coming into the world. He was in the world, and the world was made through him, yet the world did not know him. He came to his own, and his own people did not receive him. But to all who did receive him, who believed in his name, he gave the right to become children of God, who were born, not of blood nor of the will of the flesh nor of the will of man, but of God. And the Word became flesh and dwelt among us, and we have seen his glory, glory as of the only Son from the Father, full of grace and truth ... For from his fullness, we have all received, grace upon grace. For the law was given through Moses; grace and truth came through Jesus Christ. No one has ever seen God; the only God, who is at the Father's side, he has made him known.

In our previous chapter, we laid the foundation for Christianity's exclusive claim that Jesus is the Way, the Truth, and the Life according to His own words recorded in John 14:6. This chapter will expand upon that by addressing the biblical teaching concerning the deity of Christ.

Who Is Jesus?

John sets forth several attributes that point to the divine nature of Jesus Christ. First, He is *eternal*. The opening verses of John's Gospel (John 1:1-2) take us back to the beginning of creation (Gen. 1). By taking us back to Genesis, John wants us to understand that creation had a beginning, but God did not. Both the Father and the Son existed together *in eternity* prior to beginning their work of creation. And just as there was no beginning and end to God, so there was no beginning and there will be no end to Jesus, because Jesus is God (John 1:1). He is God's eternally begotten Son, who was with the Father from the beginning.

Moreover, as seen earlier, John's prologue doesn't explicitly mention the Holy Spirit, but Genesis 1:2 certainly does: "The earth was without form and void, and darkness was over the face of the deep. And the *Spirit of God* was hovering over the face of the waters" (emphasis added). The Holy Spirit is also God, eternally proceeding from the Father and the Son. Therefore, we're reminded once again of the deep and wonderous mystery of the Holy Trinity, three persons sharing one divine nature: God the Father, God the Son, and God the Holy Spirit—with no beginning and no end.[2]

The second and third attributes pointing to Jesus' divine nature reveal that He's the source of *life* and *light*: "In him was life, and the life was the light of men" (John 1:4). Human beings may produce life through procreation, but they aren't its original source; only God is. As Jesus says elsewhere: "For as the Father has life in himself, so he has granted the Son also to have life in himself" (John 5:26). Moreover, we learn that in describing God as the source of light, one author states that "John is referring to his absolute moral purity and omniscience. In other words, there is no moral defect, nor is there a lack of knowledge in God."[3] Thus, by calling Jesus the light of humanity, the apostle is putting Him on the same level as God: in character, holy; in being, omniscient (knowing all things). Only God is completely holy; only God knows all things. Therefore, only God is the source of moral purity and intelligible knowledge.

We also see something of this in Genesis 1. God speaks and light enters the darkness, bringing intelligibility, order,

---

2 For more on the Holy Trinity, see desiringgod.org/articles/what-is-the-doctrine-of-the-trinity

3 Commenting on 1 John 1:5; ligonier.org/learn/devotionals/god-is-light

and life to God's *formless* and *empty* cosmos (Gen. 1:1-3). In the same way, Jesus—the Word—enters the world He created in order to bring light and life to all who receive Him, to all who will believe in His name. Jesus doesn't come as a mere reflector of light or a guide pointing to where life might be found. He comes as the one who is light and life's very essence and source. As the apostle Paul says, "For God, who said, 'Let light shine out of darkness,' has shone in our hearts to give the light of the knowledge of the glory of God in the face of Jesus Christ" (2 Cor. 4:6).

Thus, Jesus is the answer to our deepest longings and needs, as He Himself has said: "I am the light of the world. Whoever follows me will not walk in darkness but will have the light of life" (John 8:12). And again: "I came that they may have life and have it abundantly" (John 10:10b). This means that all who live apart from Him will remain in darkness and under the sentence of death.

So, I ask you, what are those areas in your life that are dark and decaying—those things that need the light and life that only Jesus can bring? You see, Jesus can bring light and life right now, this very moment, to give you what your soul longs for, to give you life to the fullest, both now and forevermore.

Jesus is eternal. He is life and light's very essence and source; and He's also glorious. This fourth attribute may be seen in John 1:14 where we read: "And the Word became flesh and dwelt among us, and we have seen his glory, glory as of the only Son from the Father, full of grace and truth." And again, in verse 18: "No one has ever seen God; the only God, who is at the Father's side, he has made him known." This is remarkable! Why? Because we're told in the Old Testament that no one could see the face of God and live (Exod. 33:20).

But here, with the incarnation of Jesus, we have the manifestation of God's own glory before our very eyes, so that Jesus can confidently assert that "whoever has seen me has seen the Father" (John 14:9b). The glory previously ascribed to God in the Old Testament is now being ascribed to Jesus as well! He is glory incarnate, the glorious manifestation of God revealed in the Old Testament now fully manifested in the person of His Son, Jesus the Messiah, the visible expression of the invisible God!

So, we may confidently assert the deity of Jesus Christ because He is eternal. He is life and light. And He is glorious! God's Word tells us not only who Jesus is but what He does; both bear witness to His deity.

What Did Jesus Do?

John not only ascribes divinity to Jesus, but he also tells us what Jesus did. In our chapter on origins, we've seen that Jesus is the mediator of creation, the one through whom all things were created, by Him and for Him; He is the one who is before all things and in whom all things hold together (John 1:3; cf. Col. 1:16-17). It's always good to be reminded of all that Jesus did and all He does today. Think about it: the river that Jesus was baptized in was created by and for Him. The sea that Jesus calmed, created by and for Him. Even the wood of the cross, the iron of the nails, and even the hill on which He was crucified, created by and for Jesus. It's such an astounding thing to think about—that the mediator of all creation became one of us in order to save us! As was seen in the chapter on sin's problem and solution, the greatest human tragedy appeared in Genesis 3. But the good news is that God didn't leave us in our fallen condition. He promised to send a seed of the woman, and ultimately that seed is the Lord Jesus Christ, who came to reconcile us back to the Father in order that we might be reinstated as His children (John 1:11-13). From creation to the atonement to this present moment in which He is at work, Jesus confirms His deity.

Everyone Longs for a Father Who Fully Forgives
I'm reminded of an anecdote often attributed to Ernest Hemingway, about a young boy named Paco, who was living in Madrid, Spain. It's a somewhat modern version of the prodigal son where we read about Paco leaving home and wandering the streets of Madrid. His father goes to look for him but can't find him. So, he decides to put out an advertisement that read: "Paco, meet me at the Hotel Montana at noon on Tuesday. All is forgiven. Love, Papa." Well, you'd be surprised at the response. The next day, at noon, 800 young men allegedly named "Paco" showed up at the Hotel Montana. Why? Because they were longing for a father who offers full forgiveness.[4]

Only Jesus—because He's not just a man, but is the divine Son of God, truly God and truly man—has the power to reconcile us to the one we long for, the Father who fully receives and fully forgives through the redemption offered to us in His Son. This is the message of Christianity. This is the good news of Jesus Christ.

---

4   This story is popularly attributed to Hemingway, and it's often said to be from a short newspaper article he wrote titled "The Capital of the World." However, while Hemingway did write a story called "The Capital of the World" that features a character named Paco, the actual advertisement and 800 young men plot point isn't in that story. Thus, although the story is of uncertain origin, it nonetheless makes a salient point.

Practical Implications

So, what about us? For those of us who've been walking with Jesus for years and already believe that He is the God-man who came to reconcile us to the Father, let me ask you, are you surrendered to His Lordship in every area of your life? This means that Jesus is not just your Sunday morning Savior, but He's Lord of every square inch of your life. He is the Lord of your heart, mind, and soul. He is Lord of your marriage, children, and grandchildren. He is Lord of your career, finances, and ambitions. He is Lord of all!

And the same applies to young people who may be forming a new relationship with Jesus. I urge you to make it your ambition early in life to surrender all your plans, purposes, and desires to His Lordship. Ask Him for the courage to pray that He would work out His will in your life at any cost.

But perhaps you aren't a Christian. Perhaps you're reading this chapter and you agree that Jesus was one of the greatest teachers who ever lived but are having difficulty believing that He is the God-man and the Savior of the world. May I implore you to suspend your final judgment and ask Him to impress these truths on your heart? If Jesus is who He says he is, then you must either take Him at His word, or, as the great C.S. Lewis once said, dismiss Him:

> I am trying here to prevent anyone saying the really foolish thing that people often say about Him: "I'm ready to accept Jesus as a great moral teacher, but I don't accept His claim to be God." That is the one thing we must not say. A man who was merely a man and said the sort of things Jesus said would not be a great moral teacher. He would either be a lunatic—on a level with the man who says he is a poached egg—or else he would be the Devil of Hell. You can shut Him up for a fool,

you can spit at Him and kill Him as a demon; or you can fall at His feet and call Him Lord and God. But let us not come with any patronizing nonsense about His being a great human teacher. He has not left that open to us. He did not intend to.[5]

Merely calling Jesus a great teacher ignores the substance of what He taught—He claims much more. And if He's the greatest teacher who ever lived, which He is, then you must take Him at His word.

Yet, for others who may feel drawn to Jesus but are saying to themselves, "I can't become a Christian because I'm not qualified"—do you realize that the admission of *non-qualification* makes you qualified? The good news Jesus preached does not tell us to become qualified before seeking Him, but it tells us that "the kingdom of God *has come near.* Repent and believe the gospel" (Mark 1:15)! Jesus came into the world to *bring* light and life to men. He came to "proclaim good news to the poor, [to] proclaim freedom for the prisoners and recovery of sight for the blind, to set the oppressed free, to proclaim the year of the Lord's favor" (Luke 4:18-19). *Jesus* alone qualifies us to become God's children. How? Jesus qualifies us when we acknowledge that we are unqualified (repent), believe in Him, and receive Him as Savior and Lord. In fact, this is the reason John wrote his Gospel: "so that you may believe that Jesus is the Christ, the Son of God, and that by believing you may have life in his name" (John 20:31).

Jesus, Our Only Hope
Sadly, a few years ago my wife and I lost our youngest daughter, Lily. Her loss naturally prompted several questions from our children, who were five and seven. Our son would

---

5   C.S. Lewis, *Mere Christianity* (New York: Harper One, 2023), 52.

ask questions like: "How do we know for sure that we'll see Lily again? How do we know for sure that Lily's in heaven? Did she do the right things? Did she say the magic words?" Time and time again, God used this passage—John 1—to make clear the truths of the gospel and the good news that our family needed to hold on to, the truths of who Jesus is and what He has done, as our only hope of assurance that we'll see our little Lily again one day.

And it was on January 22, 2018, that my seven-year-old son traced his hand over John 1 and wrote this profession: "I believe in God." He underlined verse 12: "But to all who did receive him, who believed in his name, he gave the right to become children of God." This verse brought everything together for our family. And I hope it brings everything together for you. Not that you'll have all the answers to life's questions, but that you would come to understand that none of us earn the right to be called God's children. Only God can qualify us. And this He does through the redemptive work of His Son, Jesus Christ, our only hope.

Our family would have no hope if Jesus were simply a man. Our family would have no hope if Jesus were simply a moral example, no hope if He were just a great prophet and teacher, and you would have no hope either. But Jesus was and is more than just a man. He's the Son of God and Son of Man, the Savior and only hope for the world. This is the good news that brings the true life and light to us, as we understand that all who believe in him are given the privileged honor of becoming God's children.

For some who are reading this, today may be your day of surrender. You're invited to come to Jesus as your only hope right now. May you receive Him. May you believe in His name, and may you be given the right to become a child of God.

A Prayer of Freedom and Hope

Gracious Lord Jesus, we stand in awe before you—the eternal Word made flesh, fully God and fully man, the one through whom all things were made and in whom all things hold together. We marvel that you, who commanded the cosmos into being, would step into our broken world to rescue us. Thank you for leaving heaven's glory to take on human flesh, for living the perfect life we could not live, and for dying the death we deserved to die. We rejoice that your tomb stands empty, declaring your victory over sin and death. Lord, how often we have built walls between ourselves and you, weighed down by guilt and shame. Yet you come to us offering complete forgiveness, new life, and restored relationship with the Father. Help us to live in the freedom You purchased at such great cost. Transform us by your Spirit until we reflect your character more fully. Keep us from the twin errors of self-righteousness and despair, anchoring us instead in the confident hope of your grace. May our lives testify to your saving power, drawing others to find in you the forgiveness and purpose their hearts desperately seek. Until that day when we see you face to face, keep us walking closely with you, secure in your love, and filled with joy in your presence. In your mighty name we pray, Amen.

Application Questions

- John tells us that no one has ever seen the Father, but that Christ—the Word—is the one who makes the Father known and is the perfect revelation of God. If this is the case, does that leave us with "options" as to how we can know God? If the God who created the world has chosen Jesus, specifically, to be the way we can understand and enter into relationship with Him, what does that mean for those who say that every religion is fundamentally the same and leads to the same place?

- As we discussed in the previous chapter on sin, the effects of sin upon human nature are systemic. There is no part of us that has not been affected by sin, which means that there is no part of us that is able, on our own, to perfectly obey God as we ought. Do any of us have the power to transform our own nature? Is there anything we can do that can save ourselves? If we can't save ourselves, how might you respond to someone who feels they must clean themselves up before receiving Christ—someone who says, "I'm not qualified to become a Christian"?

- Many believe that following Jesus is about abandoning any concern for our daily lives and the state of the world. Many think that none of this down here matters. Have you heard this or thought this yourself? How would believing this affect someone's hope for today, or their desire to productively act in the world?

John, in his prologue, tells us that Jesus came in order to bring "light and life" to all who receive Him. Jesus says He came that we would "have life and have it abundantly" and that "eternal life" *is* knowing God the Father through Him (John 10:10, 17:3). Does Jesus care about the lives we are living day to day, or is it true that none of this matters? If knowing God through Christ *is* eternal life, doesn't that mean that every Christian already possesses eternal life even now? In what sense is turning to Jesus only the *beginning* of an abundant life?

- Have you heard someone say that Jesus was a great teacher, or even one of the best teachers, yet they did not follow Him? Given what Jesus claimed to be and did, does it make sense to treat Him like merely one good man among others? Consider the quote by C.S. Lewis. If Jesus did not give us the option to treat Him like just a teacher, what does this mean about our responsibility to take His claims seriously—to either reject Him outright or embrace Him fully?

- The cross is, perhaps, the starkest revelation of both the state of humanity and the character of God. On the cross, Jesus dies as a man condemned in our place, displaying the great depravity of our sin and its consequences. Yet, in the same moment, He displays God's utter love for us through His willingness to take the penalty of our sin onto Himself, so that we might be redeemed.

  Paul tells us the wages of sin is death (Rom. 6:23). Have you considered what it means that Jesus died for *your* sin? If Jesus died in order that our sin would be killed in His body, do you think your sin was brought back to life when He was raised from the dead? If God—the very Creator of the universe—was willing to die in order to save you, how should this give you hope that your sins have been forgiven, and you now have the power to walk in obedience from now on?

8

The Meaning of Life

This book has looked at several essential truths for establishing a firm foundation and a truly biblical worldview. Now as we come to the close, we will consider what Scripture says about the meaning of life.

You recall that in our chapter on origins, we approached the subject of *meaning* by answering some of life's most important questions, such as: Who am I? Where did I come from? Why am I here? Now we're going to look at the subject from a different perspective; namely, what does Scripture have to say about meaning and purpose *after* the fall of humanity (Gen. 3)? To determine this, we're going to seek wisdom from the book of Ecclesiastes.

Ecclesiastes ascribes authorship to King Solomon, the prodigal son of David (Eccles. 1:1) who, perhaps, at some point later in life came to his senses and returned to his ancestral faith. I say this because Ecclesiastes reads more like a confession—the confession of one who, in searching for meaning, tried everything "under the sun" and came up empty, only to return to his roots as the book's conclusion reveals: "The end of the matter; all has been heard. Fear God and keep his commandments, for this is the whole duty of man. For God will bring every deed into judgment, with every secret thing, whether good or evil" (Eccles. 12:13-14).

The author's prior wantonness led him down the path of skepticism. But now that the skeptic has come home, he wants other skeptics to follow. Thus, Ecclesiastes is the confession of a former skeptic writing to other skeptics in order to declare that all attempts to find meaning and purpose "under the sun" are in vain.[1] What makes him come to this conclusion? On what evidence is it based? To answer these questions, let's turn to Ecclesiastes 2–3:

> I said in my heart, "Come now, I will test you with pleasure; enjoy yourself." But behold, this also was vanity. I said of laughter, "It is mad," and of pleasure, "What use is it?" I searched with my heart how to cheer my body with wine— my heart still guiding me with wisdom—and how to lay hold on folly, till I might see what was good for the children of man to do under heaven during the few days of their life. I made great works. I built houses and planted vineyards for myself. I made myself gardens and parks and planted in them all kinds of fruit trees. I made myself pools from which to water the forest of growing trees. I bought male and female slaves and had slaves who were born in my house. I had also great possessions of herds and flocks, more than any who had been before me in Jerusalem. I also gathered for myself silver and gold and the treasure of kings and provinces. I got singers, both men and women, and many concubines, the delight of the sons of man.
>
> So, I became great and surpassed all who were before me in Jerusalem. Also, my wisdom remained with me. And whatever my eyes desired I did not keep from them. I kept

---

1 This phrase occurs twenty-nine times throughout Ecclesiastes.

my heart from no pleasure, for my heart found pleasure in all my toil, and this was my reward for all my toil. Then I considered all that my hands had done and the toil I had expended in doing it, and behold, all was vanity and a striving after wind, and there was nothing to be gained under the sun (Eccles. 2:1-11).

I hated all my toil in which I toil under the sun, seeing that I must leave it to the man who will come after me, and who knows whether he will be wise or a fool? Yet he will be master of all for which I toiled and used my wisdom under the sun. This also is vanity. So, I turned about and gave my heart up to despair over all the toil of my labors under the sun, because sometimes a person who has toiled with wisdom and knowledge and skill must leave everything to be enjoyed by someone who did not toil for it. This also is vanity and a great evil. What has a man from all the toil and striving of heart with which he toils beneath the sun? For all his days are full of sorrow, and his work is a vexation. Even in the night his heart does not rest. This also is vanity (Eccles. 2:18-23).

He has made everything beautiful in its time. Also, he has put eternity into man's heart, yet so that he cannot find out what God has done from the beginning to the end (Eccles. 3:11).

The Search for the Meaning of Life
What if someone were contracted to go on the ultimate quest in search of meaning? They would have unlimited resources. They could travel to the most exotic locations, indulging the manifold desires of their heart. They could study under the greatest of minds. But eventually they would have to report back on their findings and answer whether they had discovered the secret to life's meaning.

Well, we don't have to look very far, because Solomon has already done it for us. This is the story of a man who had it all and did it all in his quest to find the meaning of life. As alluring as Solomon's quest may appear, we can learn from his life's example and his confession in Ecclesiastes where meaning is *not* to be found.

In Ecclesiastes 2:1-8, Solomon lists the multitudinous ways he indulged in every pleasure. Did you observe the shocking admission of verse 1, where Solomon gave permission to himself to begin the quest? He says, in essence, "I told my heart: I will test you with every pleasure; enjoy yourself." From the building of houses to the planting of vineyards, gardens and parks, and from the accumulation of women to the mass accumulation of silver and gold, Solomon had everything that his mind could conceive and all that his heart desired (while apparently still holding on to wisdom, no less)! And the conclusion? All was vanity.

Now, before you say to yourself, "Pastor, I mean, this is extreme. This is extreme indulgence. I'm not like Solomon," let me challenge you by saying, "You just might be!" You see, we live in a permissive culture that promotes every form of self-indulgence and pleasure. In fact, some who are reading this may be comparing themselves with others saying, "If only I had what they have, then I'd be content. If I had just a little bit more, then I'd be happy." We are by nature creatures obsessed with self-indulgence. And why is this? When people abandon the one true God and seemingly replace Him with substitutes, they lose the only objective standard by which to discover true meaning. And at the end of the day, all they have left is their own subjectivity, a subjectivity that leads to a pursuit of the pleasures of this world.

For example, we're currently living in a time when there's little regard for unborn children, the most vulnerable in any society. If people could care less about children in the womb, then why would we be surprised when children are killed outside the womb, in atrocities such as school shootings? I say this with deep sadness in my heart. But the tragic thing is that this is what happens when a nation abandons the knowledge of God and the objective standard of His Word (cf. Rom. 1:18-32). If a person rejects the one true God who exists *above* the sun, then they are left with the only option of trying to find meaning for life *under* the sun. And the results are staggering.

The Vanity of Finding Meaning Under the Sun

Consider Solomon's perspective on the matter. In Ecclesiastes 2:11 he states, "I considered everything that I have done. I considered my work—everything that I built, everything that I made—and I realized it was all chasing the wind. I realized it was all vanity." And in verses 22-23, he says, "What has man from all the toil and striving from which he toils beneath the sun? For all the days are full of sorrow and his work is a vexation." Even at night he doesn't rest. Can you relate?

As you lay your head down on the pillow at night, does your mind race as you review everything you failed to accomplish that day? And does it race ahead in anticipation of everything you have yet to accomplish tomorrow? You see, what Solomon acknowledges is that not only has he failed to find meaning in self-indulgence, but he's also failed to find meaning in his achievements; and it's killing him. Look at his assessment of the situation.

He says things like: "What does it profit a man to work his whole life only to give it away, not knowing who will come along after me? Will they be wise, or will they be foolish?" Think about this. You work your whole life building your business, building your savings—only to give it all away, either to your children or to someone else. And you wonder, "Will they squander it all?"

But, you see, Solomon's acknowledgement is so foundational to understanding the human condition. We try to find meaning "under the sun"—through both self-indulgence and our achievements. And it kills us. It's all chasing after the wind, vanity upon vanity. You work your whole life and then you die, and a hundred years from now no one will even remember you. This is what Solomon was wrestling with.

And now, some might be thinking to themselves, "Solomon is quite the Debbie Downer." But Solomon's not being pessimistic; he's being realistic. This is the reality for everyone who seeks to find meaning in life in self-indulgence and in human achievements pursued "under the sun." So the question is this: Is it possible? If life's meaning and purpose can't be found under the sun, then where can it be found?

The Key to Finding the Meaning of Life

Well, thankfully, the answer comes in Ecclesiastes 3:11 where we read: "He has made everything beautiful in its time." What does Solomon mean by this? What he's saying is that even during those difficult times in your life, God is ultimately working everything together for the good of those who love Him, for the good of those who've found the key to life's meaning "above the sun"—namely, in God Himself. God has done this to us. "He has put eternity in [our] hearts" so that we'll never be able to find meaning apart from him. You could say that God has created us with "a hole in our hearts," an eternal void that can only be satisfied in Him alone. And as the great church father Augustine once said, and I paraphrase, we will forever be restless until we find our rest in Him.[2]

We can only find meaning, purpose, and hope by living with an eternal perspective through the lens of faith in the one who created us with this longing in our hearts. But how do we achieve this? How do we satisfy this longing in our hearts? We can't go up above the sun to achieve this eternal perspective. Read what the apostle Paul has to say in Romans 10:3-13:

> But the righteousness based on faith says, "Do not say in your heart, 'Who will ascend into heaven?' (that is, to bring Christ down) or 'Who will descend into the abyss?' (that is, to bring Christ up from the dead)." But what does it say? "The word is near you, in your mouth and in your heart" (that is, the word of faith that we proclaim); because, if you confess with your mouth that Jesus is Lord and believe in your heart that God raised him from the dead, you will be saved. For with the heart, one believes and is justified, and with the mouth one confesses and is saved. For the Scripture says, "Everyone who believes in him will not be put to shame." For there is no distinction between Jew and Greek; for the same Lord is Lord of all, bestowing his riches on all who call on him. For "everyone who calls on the name of the Lord will be saved."

We don't have to go up, because Jesus has come down. Put colloquially, He left His home above the sun in order to live below it—in order to make it possible for you and me, by faith alone, to receive life from above that we may live forever! Through Jesus' life, death, resurrection, and ascension, He has earned the right to grant eternal life to all

---

2   Augustine, *Confessions*, trans. Henry Chadwick, Oxford World Classics (Oxford: Oxford University Press, 2008), I.i.

who come to Him by faith (cf. John 10:28). This is the good news of Jesus Christ!

So, what is the meaning of life? It's to treasure Jesus above all earthly treasures because He alone is the one who satisfies the deepest longings of our hearts. It's to be assured that God the Father is pleased with us—not based on anything we have done but based on what Jesus has done for us! Jesus Christ is our greatest treasure, the one greater than Solomon (Luke 11:31), the one who is making all things new.

Do you know this Jesus? Has He captured your heart and become your Savior and Lord? Do you treasure Him above all else? If not, won't you receive Him right now—as Savior and Lord—so that you may find meaning and purpose through His redemptive work? He's the only one who can fill that hole in your heart, enabling you to live out the rest of your life with an eternal perspective and a living hope that is anchored in Him—above the sun.

If You Have Jesus, You Have Everything

A young student chose a local, state-run nursing home as his ministry during his seminary years. Every Sunday he would visit this nursing home, and one Mother's Day he brought a bunch of flowers to hand out to its female residents. On that day, he encountered a blind woman who had been living there for twenty-five years. She had no family and little if any resources. But there's something she did have. She had strong faith in Jesus Christ.

As the young man approached the woman to give her a flower, he learned that her name was Mabel. He learned also that she was blind, for upon receiving the flower she replied, "Honey, I can't see this flower. Can you wheel me down the hallway so that I can give it to someone who might truly enjoy it?" And so, the young seminarian wheeled Mabel down the hallway, and she gave it to another member of the nursing home, saying, "Here's a flower. It's a gift from Jesus."

From that point on, every Sunday when the young man visited the nursing home, he would pay a special visit to Mabel. But one day he felt a restlessness in his spirit and said to himself, "I wonder how Mabel is doing today?" He felt an urgency to find out. So he rushed over to the nursing home and found Mabel sitting in her room, where she usually was. He asked her, "Mabel, you've been on my heart and mind: What do you do all day? You have no family. You can't see anymore. What do you do all day long?" To which she replied, "Honey, I mostly think about Jesus." And she began to sing "Jesus Is All the World to Me."

> Jesus is all the world to me:
> My life, my joy, my all.
> He is my strength from day to day;
> Without Him I would fall.
> When I am sad, to Him I go;
> No other one can cheer me so.
> When I am sad, He makes me glad;
> He's my Friend.

Can you see what Mabel sees spiritually, even in her physical condition of blindness? If you have Jesus, then you have everything. This is the meaning of life: Jesus, our all-in-all.

A Prayer to Find Your All in Christ

Our God and Father, I ask you to touch the hearts of those who are reading this chapter, especially those who have been seduced by the lie that meaning and purpose are found in what they've accumulated, whether that be their wealth or achievements. May they come to realize that meaning and purpose in life are only found in the person and work of Jesus Christ.

May they look to Jesus for full forgiveness, full freedom, and say, "You've put eternity in my heart, and I acknowledge today that I will forever be restless until I find rest in you. Lord, I pray that my search for meaning would find resolution today as my heart comes to rest in the saving work of Jesus Christ—not based on any good that I have done, but solely based on Christ's finished work for me! And may this reality motivate me to live for Him and to make Him known to the ends of the earth." In Jesus' name I pray. Amen.

Application Questions

- How can you relate to Solomon? In what ways have you found yourself pursuing pleasure and meaning in the things of this world, only to find that they were ultimately disappointing? Particularly with sin, what are some of the sinful thrills you have pursued, thinking you would find great enjoyment, only to have that momentary pleasure turn to ashes in your mouth?

- Paul, writing from prison, powerfully describes the way God has taught him how "to be content," no matter the circumstance. He says "I have learned the secret of facing plenty and hunger, abundance and need—I can do all things through [Jesus] who strengthens me" (Phil. 4:11-13).

  Where do you currently lack a sense of contentment? Do you envy what others have, or are you overwhelmed by a sense that you need something more than you currently have? Take some time this week to look up your specific issues in the Bible and consider how God is calling you to change your perspective and embrace a new kind of contentment. BibleGateway.com is a useful resource to search for specific words or phrases.

- Romans 1, which has been referenced throughout this book, speaks of those who "knew God" but "did not honor him as God or give him thanks, [and] became futile in their thinking" (Rom. 1:21). Gratitude is regularly described as being central to the Christian life, recognizing that *everything* is a gift from God (Phil. 4:6; Col. 4:2; 1 Tim. 4:4, etc.).

  Would you describe yourself as a grateful person, or do you find yourself more regularly focused on your troubles? Think of a time when you were focusing on something that was causing you anxiety, constantly revisiting it in your mind. Did this help you find a productive solution? Did it bring you worse stress? What would it look like for you to spend time focusing instead on gratitude— intentionally identifying good things that you should thank God for and making the time to name those things in prayer?

- One common mistake Christians can make is in thinking that what we do down here doesn't matter at all—as if the only things worth valuing are so-called "spiritual" things (worship, prayer, Bible reading, going to church, etc.). But if treating our jobs, money, sex, etc. as if they are the ultimate value is one error, thinking that these things are inconsequential (or *not* spiritual) is an error in the opposite direction. God calls us to recognize the importance of things *in their proper place.*

Read Matthew 6:25-34. How does Jesus contrast two different approaches to life—anxious toiling vs. trusting God with gratitude? Does Jesus speak as if clothing, food, or money are unimportant? If Jesus says that we are to "seek first the kingdom of God and his righteousness, and all these things will be added to you," what does this say about your current priorities and how you ought to shift them, knowing that God promises to take care of you?

• Read Colossians 3. Paul speaks of the importance of "setting our minds on things above" rather than focusing on earthly things. What does he call "earthly" or "worldly" things? How does focusing particularly upon Jesus change our perspective toward these earthly things? What does God expect of us now that we are in Christ?

After explaining the way we are to focus on "things that are above," Paul then describes various relationships: husbands, wives, fathers, children, employees, servants, etc. How does this refute the idea that what we do down here doesn't matter? As Christians, how are we to approach our earthly responsibilities? Are you "working heartily" as if everything you do is "for the Lord and not for men" (Col. 3:23)? How would fixing your eyes on what Jesus has done help you to reframe your responsibilities in a way that encourages greater energy and dedication, without making these things your ultimate source of value?

Conclusion

A Word from the Apostle Paul

We can learn a lot from what the apostle Paul wrote to the Colossian Christians living in the first century as he addressed the cultural headwinds that were blowing in that day. They were moving further and further away from their grounding in God's Word and embracing the philosophies of the Greco-Roman culture. And so, Paul writes to inform them that Jesus Christ is not merely an addition to their worldview—He is their worldview. He doesn't just fit into their theology; He is their theology! Note Paul's numerous references to "all things" in relation to Jesus Christ as recorded in the first chapter of his letter to the Colossians:

> [Christ] is the image of the invisible God, the firstborn of all creation. For by him *all things* were created, in heaven and on earth, visible and invisible, whether thrones or dominion or rulers or authorities—*all things* were created through him and for him. And he is before *all things*, and in him *all things* hold together. (Col. 1:15-17, emphasis added)

This means that *all of life—everything in creation*—is centered in the person and work of Jesus Christ. Thus, Paul's words to the Colossians are relevant for all time as each generation seeks to build upon the firm foundation of God's Word.

Rooted in God's Word

Paul expressly states that those who've received Jesus Christ are to "walk in him, rooted and built up in him and established in the faith, just as [they] were taught" (Col. 2:6-7). This is a simple statement, but so profound. How many Christians are looking for answers to the hard questions of life? And how many are looking everywhere but in the pages of Scripture? Paul implores Christians to stick to the book—to look to the Word of God, reminding them of their roots and establishment in the faith in which they were taught, the faith that is grounded in the person and work of Jesus Christ.

This means that we don't have to walk through life blindly. We have a roadmap to help us navigate so we don't get lost. It's the Word of God, which we've been taught. And we need to be reminded of this. God has given us His Word that we might have a firm foundation on which to build. It is the final authority and the standard of truth.

This is the reason God's people gather weekly to be taught the Word of God and to be reminded of its enduring significance (Isa. 40:8). It's also why Joshua, Moses' successor, was told: "This Book of the Law shall not depart from your mouth, but you shall meditate on it day and night, so that you may be careful to do according to all that is written in it. For then you will make your way prosperous, and then you will have good success" (Josh. 1:8).

Unshaken by the World

In addition to being rooted in God's Word, Paul exhorts Christians to be unshaken by the world. In Colossians 2:8, he lists some of the ways the church was being challenged. In essence he tells them, "Don't be shaken." Or more literally: "See to it that no one takes you captive by philosophy and empty deceit, according to human tradition, according to the elemental spirits of the world, and not according to Christ." And this is so important. If we're not rooted and grounded in God's Word, we're going to be taken captive by the philosophies of our day.

The philosophers of our day can be found everywhere—from the world of academia to the world of entertainment. They promote their propaganda through various media with the intention of taking our children's hearts and minds captive. But I pray that the people of God would say, "No. Not on our watch. Not in our church. Not in this community. Neither we nor our children will be taken captive by the seductive philosophies of this world."

If you're a teenager who's reading this, please pay close attention: You will ruin your life if you follow the cultural winds wherever they go. Before you go to college and leave your home, you need to take every opportunity to be grounded in God's Word. It is imperative that you are sent out with a framework that is established in the objective truth and a faith that is unshakeable.

The God of All Grace

So the question is: How do we do this? What's the one thing that would motivate and move you to stay rooted and say "no" to the ways of the world? Well, the answer is found in Colossians 2:6. Paul says, "Therefore, as you received Christ Jesus the Lord, so walk in him." How did you receive Jesus? Paul is saying, "You received Jesus by the grace of God alone."

So the God of all grace who saved you and brought you into His family is the same God who will keep you rooted and grounded until the end. His grace connects you to His Word, and this same grace will keep you connected to Him. What this means in practice is that every day you wake up, you don't rely on your own strength, but you rely on the strength and power of God, which is the manifestation of His grace at work in your life. It's called sanctification—the God of all grace working in you so that you become more rooted and grounded in Him. The process of sanctification is nothing short of what the apostle Paul calls the renewing of your mind (Rom. 12:2).

You see, the goal of having a truly biblical worldview is not just knowing a body of content—it's coming to know the author of that content. It's not just about discovering more truth—it's coming to know that *the* truth is a person, the Lord Jesus Christ. He is the Way, the Truth, and the Life (John 14:6). So if pursuing a biblical worldview simply makes us smarter, we've completely missed the point. It should transform every area of our lives so that we're thinking and acting in accordance with God's Word. It's the God of all grace who not only brings us into His family but keeps us in His family by rooting and grounding us in a firm foundation.

Concluding Thoughts

I'm reminded of the book *All the Light We Cannot See*. It contains stories of hope during the Nazi era, a very dark time in history. It talks about light amid the darkness. One of the stories in this book is about the recruitment of young German boys into Hitler's army. The German soldiers would teach the boys to tie up prisoners and dump buckets of ice-cold water over their heads. One story recounts the experience of a Polish prisoner who was tied up in a field. There was a particular German boy who always seemed to stand out among the others. When it came his turn to take the water bucket, all the boys were cheering him on. But as he approached the prisoner, instead of dumping the icy water over his head, he dropped the bucket and said, "No, I will not do it. I will not do it."[1]

I ask you, do you have the courage to say, "I will not do it?" In this moment in history, as the cultural winds are blowing and the storm clouds are approaching, may we have the courage to stand firm on a foundation that is informed by a biblical worldview, and say, "No, I will not do it. I will not go the way of ruin and destruction." We have a firm foundation— God's very Word. We may be weak, but He is strong. Thank God that we have the solid rock on which we stand. Amen.

---

1 Anthony Doerr, *All the Light We Cannot See* (New York: Scribner, 2017).

Also available from Christian Focus ...

James ... shows us the biblical worldview. She puts God
where He ought to be—at the centre of the universe.
—**Conrad Mbewe**

THE LIES WE
ARE TOLD,
THE TRUTH WE
MUST HOLD
Worldviews and
Their Consequences

SHARON JAMES

978-1-5271-0796-0

The Lies We Are Told, the Truth We Must Hold
Worldviews and their Consequences
Sharon James

We are surrounded by lies. They are incorporated into the worldview of our culture. We daily absorb them, and these lies can have deadly effects on individuals, societies and whole civilisations.

Sharon James investigates the origins of some of these lies and looks at how we have got to the point where 'my truth' is as valid as 'your truth', and absolute truth is an outdated way of thinking. In examining the evidence of history, she highlights the consequences of applying dangerous untruths. She also looks at how Christians often respond to the culture's lies – in silence, acquiescence or celebration of them – and why these responses can be as harmful as the lies themselves.

Christian Focus Publications

Our mission statement
Staying Faithful

In dependence upon God we seek to impact the world through literature
faithful to His infallible Word, the Bible. Our aim is to ensure that the
Lord Jesus Christ is presented as the only hope to obtain forgiveness of
sin, live a useful life and look forward to heaven with Him.

Our Books are published in four imprints:

◁◯✕ CHRISTIAN FOCUS

Popular works including biographies, commentaries, basic doctrine and
Christian living.

◁◯✕ MENTOR

Books written at a level suitable for Bible College and seminary students,
pastors, and other serious readers. The imprint includes commentaries,
doctrinal studies, examination of current issues and church history.

◁◯✕ CHRISTIAN HERITAGE

Books representing some of the best material from the rich heritage
of the church.

◁◯✕ CF4KIDS

Children's books for quality Bible teaching and for all age groups:
Sunday school curriculum, puzzle and activity books; personal and
family devotional titles, biographies and inspirational stories –
because you are never too young to know Jesus!

Christian Focus Publications Ltd,
Geanies House, Fearn, Ross-shire,
IV20 1TW, Scotland, United Kingdom.
www.christianfocus.com